DATA-INFORMED LEARNERS

DATA-INFORMED LEARNERS

Engaging students in their data story

DR SELENA FISK

Copyright @ Selena Fisk 2023

All rights reserved. No part of this book may be reproduced or transmitted in any form or by any means, electronic or mechanical, including photocopying, recording or by any information storage and retrieval system, without prior permission in writing from the publisher.

Published by Amba Press
Melbourne, Australia
www.ambapress.com.au

Editor – Brooke Lyons
Cover Designer – Tess McCabe

ISBN: 9781922607522 (pbk)
ISBN: 9781922607539 (ebk)

A catalogue record for this book is available from the National Library of Australia.

Contents

Introduction		1
Part 1: Why data-informed learners?		**11**
1	Evidence-informed practice	13
Part 2: How to use data with learners		**23**
2	Purpose – why we use data with students	25
3	Mode – how we build data-informed learners	37
4	Having conversations with students	49
Part 3: Data-informed learners in practice		**67**
5	Intersection A: Goal setting and data walls	69
6	Intersection B: Goal setting and success criteria	75
7	Intersection C: Goal setting and student-generated assessment	81
8	Intersection D: Goal setting and deliberate conversations	89
9	Intersection E: Goal setting and data on walls	99
10	Intersection F: Behaviour or learner dispositions and data walls	107
11	Intersection G: Behaviour or learner dispositions and success criteria	115

12 Intersection H: Behaviour or learner dispositions and student-generated assessment 123

13 Intersection I: Behaviour or learner dispositions and deliberate conversations 129

14 Intersection J: Behaviour or learner dispositions and data on walls 141

15 Intersection K: Quality of learning and data walls 147

16 Intersection L: Quality of learning and using success criteria 155

17 Intersection M: Quality of learning and using student-generated assessment 163

18 Intersection N: Quality of learning and deliberate conversations 167

19 Intersection O: Quality of learning and data on walls 177

Conclusion **185**

About the author **189**

Acknowledgements **191**

References **193**

Introduction

The use of data in schools has gained worldwide attention and priority over the last two decades. Schools are microcosms of society, and because data permeates every other aspect of our lives, it is unsurprising that schools have become awash with data. As a result, system leaders, school leaders, middle leaders and teachers are having to rise to the challenge of using data to inform their practice, to set school improvement agendas, and to monitor progress towards achieving their goals, and their students' goals. In the worst examples of data use in schools, teachers and leaders are held almost personally responsible for student results, and some teachers are paid accordingly. However, this is not the way that data should be used. The use of data in our schools has the potential to empower more targeted teaching and learning strategies that better cater to the needs of individual students. Data can be used to demonstrate the great growth and learning that happens for individual students, small groups, classes, cohorts and schools.

While data use is an area gaining increased interest and priority for educators – largely due to policy and framing documents that influence teaching practice around the world – a key aspect of the use of school data that is often omitted from the conversation is the involvement of students. Like everything that we do as educators, we know that when we engage students in the process, we get more buy-in, are more likely to provide solutions that work for young people, and can work in partnership with students to help them achieve their goals.

Unfortunately, much of the discourse to date relates only to teachers and leaders using data for their work and their own tracking. When teachers use data that they collect on their class for their own professional practice, this has a range of outcomes for students in terms of planning, differentiation and pedagogical choices in the classroom. When middle leaders use data, they can identify trends and patterns in curriculum areas, adjust pedagogy and build capacity in their teams to cater for different student needs more efficiently. When pastoral leaders use student wellbeing, attendance and behaviour data in conjunction with learning analytics, they are provided with a fuller picture of the progress and achievement of each student. While the importance of any of these examples cannot be argued, without involving students in the process, we are missing a key piece of the puzzle. You can lead a horse to water... so they say.

To maximise the impact of our use of data in schools, we must involve students in the process. When we use data *with* students, it has a much greater impact than if they are kept out of the conversation. When data is used *with* students, it has the power to help them:

- build metacognition about how they are as a learner
- develop their understanding of their learning and achievement
- articulate their goals more clearly
- identify their current progress and challenges
- establish what they need to do to improve.

Data has the power to remove the guesswork and ambiguity of what is expected of students in terms of their learning and assessment, and our expectations and hopes for them. It provides actionable, objective, evidence-based information about their learning and progress.

The transformational power of data-informed learning

My first inkling of data's power in transforming students' learning began when I was teaching in the United Kingdom. I was Head of Physical Education. There was an expectation across the school that students had to be data-informed. (The school itself was incredibly – and negatively – driven by data, but I will share more about that distinction later.) Inspectors from the Office for Standards in Education, Children's Services and Skills (Ofsted) would regularly visit my classroom, and my students had to be able to discuss, with the inspector, their target grade for the learning area, their current working grade, and what they needed to do to improve to reach their goal. Students needed to be able to discuss why they were achieving the results they currently were, and provide specific and tangible strategies they were employing, or areas they were working on, in order to achieve their goals.

There were many aspects of the data culture in that school that were negative. Student results were used to hold teachers accountable for their actions and practice, which meant that there was a culture of fear around the potential consequences if educators did not help students reach their goals. Despite these issues with the process, students understanding their data was powerful and, indeed, transformational in my classroom. Because students knew their own data, and due to the work I did with them, they could talk openly about where they were at. They were specific in the areas they needed to improve, and they could talk genuinely about how they would reach their goals. Yes, it might be possible to perceive this negatively; however, these conversations were always conducted in a way that was supportive, pastoral, and in line with who they were as young adults and what they were aiming to achieve. The negative data-driven nature of the school more broadly was never projected onto, or shared with, students. Nor should it have been. It was about the students, their goals and what they wanted to achieve.

I very quickly noticed the positive impact that these conversations, and the tracking that I was doing of formative and summative assessments, had on students. The outcomes for these young people were profound. I saw students take greater ownership of their learning, and become agents of change. They made improvements and adjustments to what they were doing (with help and guidance from their teachers). Their consequent success in General Certificate of Secondary Education (GCSE) Year 11 subjects meant they were able to access the A-Level subjects and courses they desired at college because they achieved the results they needed to gain entry.

Having learners who were data-informed and understood the skills and knowledge they needed to improve in the subject area also supported the learning culture that I was trying to build in the classroom. If students were distracted or off-task on a given day, I was able to draw them back to why this aspect of the course was an important part of their future success. If they were disheartened with their achievement in a mock exam, I could show them the progress they had made since their previous tasks; this encouraged them not to give up. When individual student subject grade predictions increased (particularly from a D to a C grade) we made a huge deal of it and had a celebration. Students would tinker with my tracking and prediction spreadsheet, and they became creative about the ways they could build their practical performance and theory exam results. They would add a few marks here or there, seeing the difference it would or would not make, so they could establish where they could get more 'bang for their buck'. The data helped students see that they had control and agency over their learning, and it increased their motivation and engagement.

The magic of data storytelling

The use of data with students, however, isn't necessarily a common or regular practice. As a result, there is sometimes uncertainty or fear that sits around the practice – until teachers start to use data and realise its potential.

In his book *Utopia for Realists*, Rutger Bregman (2018) calls teachers 'agents of prosperity' who have one of the most influential jobs in the world due to their ability to shape human history. He states, 'If we want to change the world, we need to be unrealistic, unreasonable, and impossible.' I believe that this statement applies wholeheartedly to using data with students. It may require a leap of faith if using data with students is not common in your practice, but it can be incredibly powerful once you choose to involve students in their data story. I genuinely believe that once you try involving students in their data, the impact will snowball and you'll begin using data regularly in conversations with students.

In my work with schools as a teacher, leader and data storyteller, I am regularly reminded that data-informed learners have a host of knowledge about themselves and their learning that they may not have had otherwise. This is far more than just a student knowing a number. It's about the data but it's *not* about the data. It is about each student's understanding of the data: what it means, why it matters, how they can improve and how far they are from what they are aiming to achieve. It is the stories that the data tells students, and the narrative that sits around potential meaning and action, that makes this practice so powerful.

Data storytelling is how we bring data to life. It involves selecting the most important and impactful pieces of data, and weaving a narrative around the information to generate impact. With adults, I work through three key elements of this process that we all need to do this well; however, this approach is not limited to adults. It is useful and applicable to us and our students, if we know how to use it.

The first key element is *data literacy*: understanding what the numbers mean and what the assessments are, and whether the results are good, average or below where we would like them to be. Data literacy requires us and our students to understand the context around the numbers. The numbers themselves do not take on any meaning unless we understand the context: 'Data by themselves are not evidence of anything, until users of the data bring concepts, criteria, theories of action, and interpretive frames of reference to the task of making sense of the data' (Knapp et al. 2006). While this might be a logical piece of the puzzle, every day that I work with different schools and organisations I see assumptions being made about people's level of data literacy. It is our responsibility to level up our own understanding and work to build our colleagues' and students' data literacy.

The second important piece that we need prior to engaging in data storytelling is good *visualisations* that make the trends clear and drop the cognitive load of having to engage with raw data individually. Visualisations put 'data into forms that we can see with our eyes' (Andrews 2019), and there is a science and an art to how visualisations can be constructed most effectively (Knaflic 2015). When we use data with students, there is a range of different visualisations that might be used, including line graphs, bar charts, heat maps, box and whisker plots and scatterplots. Every one of these visualisations can be useful and helpful in ascertaining the trends and prompting thoughts about what might be next; however, like with data literacy, we often make assumptions about a user's skill in reading and interpreting visualisations. Students, especially, need these explained to them.

Good data literacy and visualisations are important foundations; however, we must get to the third and final step, *data storytelling*, for the numbers to have an impact. When we engage in data storytelling, we weave data, visualisations and narrative together so the data comes to life (Dykes 2019). To make this practical, I use two questions to guide the process:

1. What insights can I see in the data?
2. What do I do about these insights?

As teachers, we need to be able to engage in this process ourselves – it will be very difficult to engage with students about their data if we do not know how to identify insights in the first place. By building capacity in students to engage in this process, we empower them and build their capacity to be agents of their own learning.

When we are having conversations with students about their data, these two guiding questions can be a good place to start. The interesting thing about insights is that we do not all see the same things in the data, and therefore the insights we identify will be different (see Klein 2017). For this reason, it is important to have multiple perspectives looking at the data; it's vital to have students engage in this process with us. We do not ever want to lead with what *we* see in the data, or assume our insights are the only (or most important) insights. We want to ask students what *they* see and what stands out to them. Once we do this, we can prioritise the insights if we need to, and talk about what the next steps are.

Whenever we work with students and their data our focus should be on data storytelling, and getting students to a point where they are talking about action and next steps in a way that is developmentally appropriate for them. What I know, and am lucky enough to see every time this practice shows up for me in schools, is that using data with and for students can have a profound impact. Ultimately, data-informed learners:

- have a deeper understanding of their strengths
- are better able to articulate the specific areas they need to work on
- know the difference between their achievement and the progress they have made
- are more confident in talking about their progress and achievement
- have a better understanding of what is expected of them in the learning area or task
- are respectful of their peers' strengths and weaknesses and positively support others
- encourage other teachers to engage with them at the same level in the use of data.

Imagine a world in which most (or even all!) of our students were able to demonstrate these traits – not because of the numbers themselves, but because we have supported them to build their understanding and use of the numbers; they have bought into the process; and they actively engage in planning what is next for them.

At this point it is worth noting that I have seen teachers and educators using data with and for students across school sectors, with different age groups, and for students of different backgrounds. Sometimes I bump into an assumption that data is only useful for students who are in secondary school, are high performing or attend schools in affluent areas. However, that is not the case; data has the potential to work for all students – not just a select few.

About this book

This book will step you through the notion of data-informed learners, and provide you with ideas and examples that you might like to use or adapt to your own context.

Part 1 details why data-informed learners are more successful learners, and how using evidence enhances our teaching practice. Using data is possible (and useful) in conversations about both progress and achievement, and the final section in part 1 unpacks this distinction.

Part 2 discusses the ins and outs of using data with students. There are three key reasons (or *purposes*) for using data with students, and five ways (or *modes*) through which this can be done; all are discussed in this section. There are important factors to think about in terms of your approach to having data conversations with students, and these are outlined in the latter section of part 2.

Having set up the thinking about how, when and why we can use data with students, part 3 investigates 15 intersections between purpose and mode. There are countless ways that these intersections play out in different classrooms; a couple of examples have been provided in each area of overlap, to highlight possible opportunities to use data with students and create data-informed learners.

Like my two previous books that are specific to schools, *Using and Analysing Data in Australian Schools* and *Leading Data-Informed Change in Schools*, I hope that this resource provides you with prompts and ideas on how you can actively develop data-informed learners in your school or classroom. I hope it inspires you with concepts you can adapt and develop to suit the needs of your context and your students. No two classrooms, teachers or students are the same; resources such as this rely on you establishing what might work for you, but provide the prompts and frameworks through which to come up with your own awesome ideas. There is not a huge amount written in the area of data-informed learners, so my hope is that this resource furthers the conversation and provides an opportunity for others to build on these ideas and this practice. I hope you have so much fun with it.

PART 1

Why data-informed learners?

In the mid 1800s there was a series of cholera outbreaks in London. Most believed, as per the miasma theory of the time, that cholera was an airborne disease. Physician John Snow, however, theorised that the disease was carried in water. In the 1854 outbreak, he set out to track the evidence that he could access of the cases of cholera in the Soho area. He famously visually depicted the locations of cases in the community to establish that the Broad Street water pump was the source of infection, and proved that the disease was, in fact, waterborne (Tulchinsky 2018). Over the subsequent decades, Snow's findings contributed to the development of germ theory, and measures were put in place that ultimately decreased the prevalence of cholera and large-scale morbidity around the world. These measures have been 'responsible for nearly half the total mortality reduction in major cities, three-quarters of the infant mortality reduction, and nearly two-thirds of child mortality reduction' (Tulchinsky 2018).

John Snow's mission to ascertain the real source of infection is a great example of evidence-informed practice with a focus on action. Snow started out with a hypothesis; then he actively sought evidence about the people who contracted the disease, looked for trends in the data and identified the problem. As a result of this work and his findings, actions were taken that had a significant impact – not only on people in London, but all around the world.

In schools, and as educators, we have access to so much evidence. We have quantitative data from standardised assessments, diagnostic assessments, in-class summative and formative tasks, attendance registers and wellbeing surveys. We have (possibly even more) qualitative data from student work samples, observations, anecdotal learnings, conversations with colleagues and parents, and categorical and open-ended survey questions. We are not short of evidence.

If John Snow had kept the Broad Street pump insight and evidence to himself (or let it hide in a spreadsheet on a computer!) he would never have been able to alert local residents to the dangers in the water supply. The people of London would have continued to believe that cholera was an airborne disease, they would have continued doing what they always did, and they would not have been able to take tangible action that actually made a difference to whether or not they contracted cholera.

For me, there are so many parallels between the story of John Snow and the notion of data-informed learners. When we are transparent about the data, and when we share the information with people who can actually act on it, we can have a significant impact – and it can ultimately benefit a lot more people than if the data had not been shared.

In the following pages, you will have the opportunity to think about evidence versus action and where you and your team are positioned. We'll then talk about the importance of involving students in their data story, and the important distinction to be made between progress and achievement measures and uses.

Chapter 1

Evidence-informed practice

In schools, we have access to a lot of evidence – both in-school learner data and research evidence – and we all access or rely on this evidence at varying levels and at different times. Some practitioners use evidence extensively in their work, others less so; we all fit somewhere on a continuum from using very little, to a lot.

In addition to thinking about the amount of evidence we use in our work, we can also think about the action that we take. Do we tend to innovate and try new things, or do we continue to do what we have tried (and tested) before? Like with the amount of evidence we use, we all sit somewhere on a continuum of people who are incredibly innovative and reflexive, to people who choose to do the same thing, year in, year out.

The notion of these two continuums – action and evidence – can be conceptualised in the four-quadrant model shown in figure 1 (from Fisk 2022a). We all fit into one of the four quadrants, depending on how much evidence we use and the type of action we take. The quadrant categories are: statis, guess work, lost opportunity and impact. John Snow would undoubtedly fit into the 'impact' quadrant – he collected evidence and took action as a result of it.

Figure 1: Evidence versus action quadrant (from Fisk 2022a)

At times we may move around the quadrant model, moving further left or right or up or down – perhaps even moving across an axis into a new quadrant. Our colleagues, teams and schools can all be positioned on this model. Have a think about where you sit, as well as where the people you work with every day might sit.

Thankfully, I have not met many teachers, teams or schools in the 'statis' quadrant. People in this quadrant use very little evidence and do not take action or modify their practice. Given the amount of data and evidence we have in schools, it is almost impossible for anyone to be in this quadrant – unless, of course, they choose to completely ignore all of the evidence that is available! Given school improvement initiatives are often led by systems and boards, there is always a focus on improvement and what might come next, meaning that the notion of staying the same, at a school level, is almost unheard of.

There are some educators (and schools) who, at times, fit in the bottom-right quadrant: 'guess work'. Although there is a lot of learner data, as well as research evidence to indicate which strategies might work better than others, sometimes people make the mistake of trying something new without evidence to support their decision-making. If we try something out, without the evidence to know whether our students need it or whether it could possibly be an effective program, we really are guessing as to whether or not the change will have an impact. People in this quadrant may be trying their best, and trying to do something good for their students and community, but they don't know what they don't know. It is my hope that with support and professional learning, people, teams and schools in this quadrant can begin to collect and use more evidence to inform their decision-making and move into the 'impact' quadrant.

Many teachers, teams and schools fit into the quadrant on the top left: 'lost opportunity'; in fact, people in this quadrant make up the largest proportion of those I work with. These are educators and schools who have access to a lot of evidence, but they do not necessarily act on it. There can be a number of reasons for this:

- They do not understand all the evidence they have access to (such as standardised assessment) and are reluctant to make changes based on their limited understanding.
- They understand the data but are unsure how to use it.
- They know what they want to try but do not have the resources or support they need.
- They are worried about making a change and getting it wrong.

All of these scenarios are okay (and very common), but the challenge is to help people and school communities move from 'lost opportunity' into 'impact'. Educators who are in the 'lost opportunity' quadrant should be supported to help them see how they can implement action and shifts in practice that respond to the evidence they have.

The aim is to be in the 'impact' quadrant, where we collect accurate and reliable evidence and act accordingly. There are certainly many teachers, teams and schools who proudly sit in this category. Educators in this quadrant act on the evidence and data that they have access to (that is, both in-school data and research evidence), and respond in a way that is informed by the data and what research tells them about the most effective interventions. Imagine if every classroom could be filled with students who are heard and whose unique skills and needs are known, and teachers who do everything they can to act on those strengths and gaps. Action people in this quadrant take may not always be as successful as they might have liked (after all, nothing ever goes perfectly when we are trying new things), but they continue to review the evidence and adapt where they can to maximise the impact they have on their learners.

Involving students in the conversation

Given the worldwide focus on using research evidence and other data in schools, at this point you are probably well versed in why data is important and useful for educators, and how it can positively impact your classroom, year level, department and school. However, while there is increasing work being done in this space, there is less emphasis in the literature on engaging students in the process and involving them in conversations about their data. I have seen countless examples of this working well. I strongly believe that it is not until we bring students along on the journey with us that we will truly have the data-informed impact we hope to.

In the description and discussion of figure 1, I focused on educators – what evidence we use and how we act on it. However, this is not limited to us – the same model and thinking applies to students. Ultimately, we want students to be in the impact quadrant too. This is where they use evidence of their progress and achievement and have access to their data, and they are supported to think about what that might mean for them and what they can do about it.

While there might be limited literature about students acting on their own data and learning analytics, we do have definitive evidence about the power of feedback. The notion of feedback has gained significant attention since Black and Wiliam's seminal work in 1998, which outlined its considerable impact on student achievement. Education academic John Hattie stated that feedback has an effect size of 0.7, which is higher than many other school-based factors, and more impactful than many other strategies investigated in his meta-analyses (Visible Learning 2022). Even though effect sizes are not perfect – they are an average, and based on varying numbers of studies – the literature (and common sense) tells us that some types of feedback are more helpful and effective than others. For example, specific, future-focused, practical strategies are more effective than feedback that focuses on praise and encouragement.

Further, the literature reminds us that feedback that is provided on formative tasks – and, more specifically, feedback that is used formatively – enables students to act on feedback; to make adjustments to their product, process or study habits to achieve better results. This is more effective than feedback on summative assessment, which they will probably never do again. Of course, there is some feedback that can be generated from that assessment that could be effectively used as formative feedback, but the grade itself does not tell students how to improve.

We know feedback works for students. However, in the school data space, where teachers generate so much data on student formative and summative tasks, a lot of it often does not make its way back to students, or students are not involved in a conversation about their performance. There are many uses of data that do not require this feedback loop to be closed; however, there are many benefits if and when it is. Closing the loop with data is no different to any other feedback that we provide to students on their performance, such as us being proud of a performance, acknowledging when they do something nice for a student, or commending them for improvements in attitude. But when students are engaged in the process, they can contribute to the conversation, reflect on their progress and feel as though they own their steps forward.

We also know that assessment in schools is changing from the traditional assessment model to a new model. In 2016, Cope and Kalantzis did a good job of conceptualising this emerging assessment model in the era of big data and comparing it to the traditional assessment model, highlighting some of the key differences between the two (table 1). They identified a shift from assessment being external to the learning process, to being embedded in learning. It is not something that is done *to* students, but something that they are a part of. There is a renewed focus on implementing and using good formative assessment, as we know that is where we can actually work with students to make a change. But most importantly for this discussion, the comparison highlights that both students and teachers use and analyse student data in this emerging model; in fact, both are 'data analysts' with the help of dashboards and visuals. In my work, I have seen this done well, where all of these themes of the emerging model are present, and students are motivated and engaged: they know their data, set goals and make improvements.

Table 1: Traditional compared to emerging models of assessment (from Cope and Kalantzis 2016)

Traditional assessment model	Emerging assessment model
Assessment is *external* to learning processes; the challenge of 'validity' or alignment of the test with what has been taught	Assessment is embedded in learning; 'validity' no longer a challenge
Limited opportunities for assessment, *restricted data sets* (select and supply response assessments)	Data are big because there can be *many small data points* during the learning process (structured and unstructured data)
Conventional focus on *summative assessment*	Renewed focus on *formative assessment*
Summative assessment is an outcomes or *end view* of learning	Summative assessment is a progress view, using data that were at first formative to trace learning progressions; feedback is *recursive*
Expert or teacher assessors	*Crowdsourced*, moderated assessments from multiple perspectives, including peers and self
Focus on *individual memory* and deductions leading to correct or incorrect answers	Focus on knowledge representations and *artifacts* that acknowledge textual provenance and trace peer *collaborations*
Assessment of *fact and correct application*	Assessment of *complex epistemic performance*, disciplinary practice
Assessment experts as *report grades*	Learners and teachers as data analysts, with the support of *analytics dashboards and visualizations*

In his book *Drive* (2011), Daniel Pink discusses what motivates humans in the work environment, beyond consequences and rewards. He says that once we feel we are paid well for our work, we need three things to be motivated:

- purpose
- autonomy
- mastery.

Pink argues that these factors impact motivation at home and school, as well as work. He makes the case that when we can provide all three conditions and opportunities, people (read: students) are motivated to engage, work hard and succeed.

I raise his work at this point because I believe the use of data with students feeds into all three of these elements. Students who set realistic goals have an idea of where they are headed and what they contribute to their trajectory; they have a clearer sense of purpose. When students see the way their learning is assessed and understand what is required to achieve, they build their autonomy as learners. When they see their results improve and see that their hard work has paid off, they develop mastery, begin to see how rewarding it is and learn that success is possible.

Progress and achievement

One point I often make with teachers when I talk about using data to inform their pedagogical decisions is that it's important to distinguish between *progress* measures and *achievement* measures. Both are powerful indicators of what students might need in terms of teaching and learning, and when we bring students into these conversations, this distinction is equally important and both messages are equally powerful.

Achievement measures are those that 'score' a student and provide feedback on their level of skill or understanding, or their performance in a particular task. As teachers, we generally do achievement measures well: we assess work against the curriculum standards, mark exams and give scores and percentages, or review scores on standardised assessments. All these examples are achievement measures, as they are point-in-time, one-off results that represent where a student is at. Both formative and summative results might fall into the category of achievement measures – in this case, the assessment type is less important than the individual nature of the result.

On the other hand, *progress* measures reflect student achievement over time, and require two or more measures so the distance moved can be considered. Progress calculations generally rely on achievement results, but the focus is on the growth from past result to current result, rather than the value of the most recent achievement. For example, in a weekly spelling test, if a student went from achieving 5 out of 10 to 7 out of 10 to 8 out of 10, the student improved by three points – from 5 to 8. Alternatively, if a student went from a score of 45 per cent in a pre-test to 71 per cent in the post-test, they improved by 26 percentage points.

In the context of developing data-informed learners, both progress and achievement conversations are important, as they both provide an opportunity for growth and reflection. Even when achievement is high, the student may not have performed well compared to their previous result; if their result is average, but it's their highest result to date, that is worth knowing and celebrating. These occurrences would lead to two very different, yet relevant, conversations with students.

Both progress and achievement data can be used when engaging with students in all of the examples in part 3 of this book. However, the conversations will have a different focus. For progress data, the conversation is led by talking about the areas in which the student is improving, and the difference in improvement in some areas versus others. This is powerful as it provides context around whether the student's results are getting better, are lower than previously or match past results. This gives feedback to the student as to whether or not their actions are helping them improve. This can be more useful information than a single result that is not framed in the context of previous achievement.

The next step worth thinking about is why and how we involve students in this work with their data. In part 2, you will learn about the three reasons why we use data with students, and the five modes by which this can be done. Chapter 4 considers some common challenges and concerns with the use of data with students and gets you to reflect on your confidence and skill in having conversations with students around their data. It also provides tips to make the process easier and ultimately more successful.

PART 2

How to use data with learners

By using data with and for students, we bring them into the space where they can be agents of change in their own learning. Students should be involved in conversations with their data, as it can contribute to their motivation and drive – giving them what Daniel Pink (2011) refers to as 'purpose, mastery and autonomy'. Involving students in data helps them answer the three key questions of effective feedback, as identified by Hattie and Timperley (2007):

1. Where am I going? (What are the goals?)
2. How am I going? (What progress is being made towards the goal?)
3. Where to next? (What activities need to be undertaken to make better progress?)

There are two main categories to consider when thinking about using data with and for students to develop data-informed learners. The first is *purpose* – this is the reason why we would engage students in this process and want to develop learners who are data-informed. There are generally three purposes for using data with students: for goal setting, for behavioural or learner dispositions information, or to review the quality of learning, skill or understanding.

The second category to consider is the *mode* through which data is used with students. The five modes by which this most commonly occurs are: data walls, the use and co-construction of success criteria, student-generated assessment, deliberate conversations, and data on walls in classrooms.

When considered in a table format, as per table 2, we can see there are 15 intersections in which the purpose and the mode meet. All modes can be used for all purposes, but there are some intersections that we rely on more than others and use more often. We will discuss and unpack the 15 intersections in part 3 of this book, which provides some examples of the ways you might use these modes and purposes to develop data-informed learners in your school or classroom.

Table 2: Intersections of purpose and mode for data-informed learners

		Purpose		
		Goal setting	Behaviour or learner dispositions	Quality of learning
Mode	Data walls	A	F	K
	Success criteria	B	G	L
	Student-generated assessment	C	H	M
	Deliberate conversations	D	I	N
	Data on walls	E	J	O

In the remaining sections of part 2 we'll unpack the three purposes of data-informed learners, and the modes through which this can be done. The final section discusses the ways in which we can have these conversations with students in the most effective manner.

Chapter 2

Purpose – why we use data with students

Before discussing the ways in which we can develop data-informed learners, it is important to unpack the three different reasons my we might use data with students. We always need a 'why' for what we do (check out Simon Sinek's 2009 work on the 'why'); using data with and for learners is no different.

Ultimately, the reason we want to use data with students is so we can better support them to succeed – in whatever way, shape or form that looks like. We use data in a way that is deliberate and effective, supporting students by providing a structure and process by which they can engage and improve.

Generally, there are three main reasons to use data with students; let's take a closer look at each of them now.

Goal setting

The first of three reasons for using data with learners is for the purpose of goal setting. As adults, we know the importance of goal setting in our own work and lives; as teachers, we know that students having clear goals is no different. In some ways, this is a reason why learning intentions and success criteria have become so heavily recognised for their impact (when used well) and are used across schools – they help identify a clear focus and outcomes for the lesson, and make the 'goal' and intended outcomes of the lesson more visible, for both the teacher and student. John Hattie's meta-analysis of influences on student achievement indicate that the impact of having a learning goal versus not having a learning goal is 0.68 (Visible Learning 2022).

More broadly, though, research indicates that goal setting is critical to making improvements and reaching new heights in all aspects of our lives. From a personal perspective, I have my own goals and aspirations; having these undoubtedly means I think about what I am going to do to achieve them. I set out a plan – and while it is not perfect, it means that I am more likely to achieve what I set out to do. In terms of students and our schools, 'appropriately challenging goals' has an effect size of 0.59 (Visible Learning 2022), which puts this in the top quarter of the factors that John Hattie includes in his work.

In many ways, there is a lot of goal setting that happens in classrooms – both formal and informal. For the purposes of this book, I will focus on the more formal ways of setting goals, as there is a range of different factors and elements that contribute to the informal (and sometimes intangible) goal-setting conversations, comments and feedback that we provide students daily. Things like having students complete a task before they are allowed to go to lunch, giving them a choice about their behaviour and possible consequences, and helping a student get to class on time, could all, in some way, be perceived has helping students set a goal and stick to a plan.

With respect to formalised goal-setting procedures, however, there are different ways that we can engage in goal setting with students. These include:

- In a one-on-one conversation with students about their learning, behaviour, attendance, wellbeing and so on.

- In a three-way conversation with the student and their parent/guardian, in either a scheduled meeting or parent-teacher interview.
- As a class activity, where students are stepped through the process of writing a goal for the subject area, time period, assessment item or skill.

When these goals are constructed, they could be stored:

- in the student's classbook or online notebook
- on the teacher's tracking sheet or record-keeping document
- on a wall in the classroom showing all student goals
- in a school learning analytics dashboard against the student file.

Different approaches and strategies will work for different teachers and students at different times, and that is okay. This is about identifying an approach that suits you and your context. In saying that – irrespective of the way the goals are constructed and where the information is kept – it is important, when planning the way the goal setting will occur, to think through and discern the purpose of this activity, and what you hope your students will get out of it. You need to ensure that it is a process that is purposeful and effective for students, rather than something that does not get a good return on investment.

Process versus outcome goals

An issue that I have experienced often, and know many teachers grapple with, is students who set goals that are too broad and not specific enough; or goals that are focused solely on an *outcome* rather than the *process*. Research indicates that process goals are more effective than outcome goals, but developmentally shifting from process to outcome goals is the most effective of all (see Zimmerman and Kitsantsas 1997). Rather than students aiming for a specific outcome (which might be good if they get there, but is not helpful in getting them to think about *how* they might achieve it), we need them to identify steps to improvement, and help them progress these goals as they improve.

When I think of broad outcome goals the example that comes to mind for me is the goal-setting process my nephew, Jhye, went through at his secondary school. He engaged in the goal-setting activity on his own, and I was sent an automatically generated email from the school after he had entered his goals. He had developed six goals for himself, all of which were too broad and completely outcomes oriented:

1. To achieve a B in English
2. To achieve a B in Maths
3. To achieve a C in Science
4. To achieve a C in Religion
5. To achieve a B in Geography
6. To achieve a B in Information and Communication Technology (ICT).

Given that, at the time, he was failing half his subjects and probably did not have the self-regulation or motivation to make the changes needed to jump whole grade boundaries, these goals did not serve his needs, nor did they help him improve. He was aiming for significant (and, at the time, impossible) improvements in every subject he was studying, without the skills in his toolkit to make the changes he needed to.

When I think of specific goals that are developmentally appropriate, I think about the teachers I worked with at a primary school in Sarina, northern Queensland. Teachers across the school had very specific goals for their students in literacy and numeracy. However, the example from the prep classroom stood out to me.

The teacher had co-constructed goals with each student. One student's goals were:

- Count past 100
- Count backwards from 20 to 0
- Count in 5s and 10s.

These goals were a manageable difficulty, and they were tangible in that the student could clearly see whether they reached their goal or not. The fact that these goals were not the same for all students meant that they were developmentally appropriate and unique for each learner.

Progress versus achievement goals

When we set goals with students, they are often related to reaching a particular level of achievement, or being able to do something new. An achievement goal might be to average 8 out of 10 spelling words correct each week. However, there is also a lot of opportunity to set progress goals as well. Rather than focusing on only the outcome, progress goals focus on the improvement a student hopes to make. For example, improving from an average of 8 out of 10 to 9 out of 10, or aiming to double a score on a post-test compared with a pre-test result, are both examples of progress goals. Both progress and achievement goals are useful, and relevant at different times.

Reviewing and refreshing goals

It is important to regularly review and refresh goals, so students know where they are at. This is your opportunity to talk with them about where they feel they are going well and any challenges they are having. You can celebrate and recognise achievements regularly, and reset new goals where required. Goals only work for young people when we circle back to them, talk about them regularly and remind them of what they have achieved.

Teachers and schools that I have seen do this well are having regular goal-setting conversations with students. In the example of the prep classroom provided previously, the teacher was having goal-setting conversations with students a couple of times per term. In my nephew's more formalised goal-setting mentoring set-up, he had goal-setting conversations with his mentor each term. When I worked as a mathematics teacher, I had goal-setting conversations with students whenever their data indicated that I needed to; meaning that weekly, I was talking with at least one student about what they were aiming for and how their behaviour and engagement did (or did not) match their goals.

If you ask students to construct goals at the beginning of the year or semester but then allow them to languish, you do not create buy-in, student agency or improvement. You also miss a massive opportunity to celebrate the progress that students make if and when they do achieve what they set out to.

Behaviour or learner disposition information

The second of three reasons why we might use data with students is to provide feedback or information on their behaviour or learner dispositions. In terms of behaviour, this could be quantitative, such as:

- the number of behaviour incidents
- the severity of different behaviours
- incident tallies related to teachers, lessons, times of the day or areas of the school
- the number and type of positive behaviours for learning

- scores on behaviour cards that have been entered by teachers
- the number and type of detentions, timeouts, Responsible Thinking Centre (RTC) referrals and so on.

There is also a lot of qualitative data available on student behaviour, including:

- behaviour comments and reports entered on behaviour management platforms
- emails detailing incidents that have occurred
- notes from meetings with students, parents or colleagues
- observations of student behaviour and interactions with their peers
- notes and comments on behaviour cards.

All of these different types of data could be used with students, and could be beneficial in helping students understand how they are progressing and where they can improve.

Learner dispositions data is a much more complex than behaviour data, largely because it is being collected and considered in a relatively new way. Teachers have long given learner disposition scores at reporting time on things like homework completion, effort and behaviour, on a scale such as a 1–5 scale. In some instances, these scores are aggregated for specific subjects, or across the student's subjects. They can also be used to consider cohort, subject or year-level trends.

More recently, some schools have tried to track and report learner dispositions on a rubric of skill, including elements such as resilience, engagement, respectful relationships, collaboration and so on. While there are levels of cross-curricular priorities and general capabilities in documents such as the curriculum, many schools are looking for more generic, translatable and reportable ways of tracking and utilising this data.

One resource I have seen schools use to help track dispositions is the '5 levels of student engagement' model published on the TeachThought website by Founder and Director, Terry Heick (2022), based on work by Phillip C Schlechty (2002). The five levels of engagement are:

1. engagement
2. strategic compliance
3. ritual compliance
4. retreatism
5. rebellion.

Each level has a descriptor, which we will discuss in more detail in intersection I later in this book.

I have seen schools use the levels exactly as they are, and others that have adapted them using language that is more contextually appropriate for their school. Some schools use a framework like this for teachers to give students a score on their learner dispositions, some have students self-reflect and self-report using this scale, and some collect both data from students and teachers and compare the results.

Another example of a scale that is used by some schools is the BEST for the Future 'Self-Direction Toolkit' (2022). This framework includes levels for a range of learner dispositions, and (unlike the TeachThought model) shows different levels and expectations for different year levels. There are rubrics assigned to K–2, 3–5, 6–8 and 9–12, and each has an aspirational level that students 'should' be working at. I have seen this toolkit used for students to self-assess, for teachers to score students, and for both to score and then have a conversation to agree on an outcome.

The notion of tracking learner dispositions and behaviour is not new, but the formalisation and triangulation of it alongside traditional learning analytics is.

Quality of learning or level of understanding

The final, and most common, way to use data with students is in the realm of learning analytics: to provide information about the quality of student work, level or skill, or depth of understanding. This is the purpose with which you are possibly most familiar; after all, we have marking and reporting obligations to parents and students, as outlined by our government departments and curriculum. It is what we learn at university – we learn to understand the curriculum and levels, and we are shown how to mark and provide feedback to students.

The nuance here, however, lies in the way in which we use data with students. You may have had the experience of a student saying that they didn't look at their most recent report card; or, if your school releases online report cards, you may have found that some parents do not log in or view what is written. In some ways, I don't blame them – many report comments are generic; students generally have a good idea of how well they have achieved prior to the report being released; and there is often not much value in the feedback provided on assessments that students will never do again. We explored in part 1 that the power of feedback lies in formative rather than summative feedback (see Black and Wiliam 1998); report cards are a good example of why summative feedback is not as effective as the other options in our toolkit.

Students can make changes when they are provided with effective formative feedback. The more specific we can be in this feedback, and the more we use specific data and evidence in this feedback, the better understanding students have of where they are at, where they are trying to get to and what they need to do to improve. This data might come from formative tasks such as quizzes, practice tasks and student work samples, or summative results, predictions or drafts. Either way, using data in a way that is formative makes the process clearer and more specific to students.

When I was teaching senior Physical Education, I regularly used A–E levels in drafting feedback, and during practical lessons throughout the term. When I marked drafts of written assessments, I would provide feedback that compared their work to the criteria. I would make comments such as:

> *If I were to mark this work now against the criteria, you would receive an A for acquire, a B for apply and a B for evaluate, because while you have demonstrated a very high level of understanding, you haven't yet applied the knowledge to the sport of badminton, or evaluated your own performance at the same level.*

I did this because students wanted feedback on the quality of their work. Ascertaining the difference in highly nuanced language in the criteria was usually difficult for students, and the A–E level system was a type of data that they easily understood and connected with.

However, at the time that I was teaching, the English syllabus specifically stated that A–E grades should not be used when drafting student work, so I understand that this approach is not for everyone! But I felt this process worked well for me and for my students. I used language that was specific to the criteria that they were being marked against, and when we discussed practical performance, we talked openly about student performance at different grades, and about the difference between an 'A' performer and a 'B' performer. Students became more articulate about their own skills and what they were working on; and in the practical lessons, they could visibly see a model of the student performance grade that they were aiming for.

There is a lot of scope for using this type of data with students at this time, however there are also countless opportunities for using formative tasks, summative feedback and standardised assessment information with students. Opportunities to have conversations with students about their performance in a subject over time, comparison of grade point averages (GPAs) over time, or looking at achievement or growth in standardised assessments can also be incredibly useful. This can be done in different ways and at different times. We'll unpack some examples of these practices in part 3.

This chapter has considered the three main reasons why we might use data with students: to help with goal setting, to provide information about behaviour or learner dispositions, and to provide feedback on the quality of learning or level of understanding. There are five modes, or ways in which we might do this, and these are unpacked in the following chapter.

Chapter 3

Mode – how we build data-informed learners

When we talk about how to build data-informed learners, there are five main modes by which we can do so. They are:

- data walls
- success criteria
- student-generated assessment
- deliberate conversations
- data on walls in classrooms.

There is no right or wrong way to engage students in their data, and all modes have different uses and relevance at different times. Some strategies will work for some teachers and some students better than others at different times. All of that is okay; it is about finding the mode that works best for you and suits your context – and, ultimately, giving it a go!

Data walls

Lyn Sharratt and Michael Fullan (2012) are well known for the notion of 'putting faces on the data' and using data walls. Data walls are a high-impact strategy for improving student achievement, as they humanise the data and remind us that the numbers represent individual students' achievement. Without faces on the data, we tend to focus on the numbers rather than the humans who should ultimately be benefiting from our analysis and data discussions.

There are a number of ways that data walls can be constructed. They are focused on a particular aspect, such as reading, writing, numeracy or attendance. Some data walls show achievement and the different levels that students are at, whereas others show and highlight the growth or movement that students have achieved. Others combine achievement and progress, and highlight student results and the movement they have made since the previous assessment. Data walls are often located somewhere in a staff area, and usually incorporate a method of covering the data if needed for privacy – for example, using sliding doors, roller blinds or positioning them on a moveable board.

Where possible, data walls should triangulate information on the students with at least three relevant data points, rather than solely representing a single type of data or single data point. This is usually done on the data card itself. Triangulating information is an important approach when using data, and the inclusion of this practice on data walls is no different. If, for example, a data wall focuses on writing, the data card might show a writing task result from English, the most recent standardised writing assessment result and a peer comparison. Students' faces might be positioned on the data wall based on one of these data points, but they are all recorded on the card and visible to the user.

Data walls are useful when they are used well, and that is done best when teachers regularly engage with the information, and contribute to the construction of the wall and the moving and updating of the cards. Data walls are, however, time-consuming to construct. They also run the risk of becoming relics in the school if their use is not authentically embedded in other school processes. They are, after all, not a high-yield strategy if they are not used!

Although it is not hugely common practice to use these resources with students (and you would not do it all the time), there are some examples, as we'll unpack in part 3, where they can be useful resources to prompt and guide conversations with students about their learning.

Success criteria

There is a lot of research that talks about the impact of learning intentions and success criteria. (I've worked in a lot of schools where there was an expectation that they were shown on the board at all times, regardless of how well-written they might have been!) Learning intentions are often statements that are directly related to the curriculum. They state what the students should know or be able to do by the end of the lesson (Australian Institute for Teaching and School Leadership n.d.). Robert Marzano makes the distinction between procedural and declarative knowledge, and this is often the lens through which learning intentions are written (Marzano 2007).

Success criteria, I believe, are hidden gems in this relationship. These criteria are designed to outline what success looks like for students: what they will be able to do once they have mastered the learning intentions (see Australian Institute for Teaching and School Leadership n.d.). Success criteria are *not* a list of activities for students to complete; rather, they are statements describing what they can do and how well they can do it. This is a common misconception I have seen in schools. When I taught in the United Kingdom, there was an expectation that we would have three levels of success criteria for all lessons. They used a generic formula:

- By the end of the lesson all students will be able to...
- By the end of the lesson most students will be able to...
- By the end of the lesson some students will be able to...

In some ways, these were aligned with 'C', 'B' and 'A' students, but it wasn't quite that simple. It was not a perfect example of the use of success criteria, but it was better than having a list of tasks to complete.

Success criteria are most impactful when students don't merely copy them into their books, but are involved in their construction. When students are involved in deciding what success looks like and the different levels of proficiency, they have greater buy-in – they understand what is expected of them, and what to aim for. Good success criteria clarify the expectations, and student understanding of the expectations is unpacked and expanded during a co-construction process. If students are given success criteria that are already formed, rather than being involved in their development, they will not have the same depth of understanding or buy-in.

The examples provided in part 3 on building data-informed learners relate predominantly to co-constructed success criteria. Although co-constructing success criteria is time-consuming and you would not go through this process every lesson, or for every unique learning intention, it can be worth engaging in this process for longer-term learning intentions or goals.

A common example that Lyn Sharratt refers to, and one that I have seen myself, is the co-construction of success criteria for writing a sentence. In this example, the teacher talks to students about working on writing a sentence, and they discuss what 'success' might look like. The success criteria become something along the lines of the following:

A good sentence:

- starts with a capital letter
- ends with a full stop
- has finger spacing in between the words
- makes sense when I read it out loud
- includes words from the vocabulary lists around the room.

Students and teachers together develop this list and it is published on the classroom wall as a reference for students. This conversation can be incredibly powerful, as it relates to a skill that students are working on over a number of weeks.

In practical subjects, co-constructing success criteria is often done explicitly by unpacking elements of a successful final 'product'. In Physical Education, for example, an effective badminton smash shot is when:

- the player hit the shuttle at the highest point
- the player's hitting arm is fully extended
- the shuttle and racquet contact occurs just in front of the body
- the player is at maximum height from the ground
- rotation comes through the legs, torso and shoulders
- the hitting arm follows through
- the shot trajectory is steep and into space.

This list could be co-constructed with students by watching a slow motion video of a highly effective smash, or by watching a capable student in class. This is a skill that students might work on over a number of weeks or throughout the unit of badminton, meaning that the success criteria would stay the same throughout.

As the unit (and student skill) progresses, students can self-assess against the success criteria. They have clear actions to improve, and know more clearly where their skill level aligns.

Student-generated assessment

While it's not on everyone's radar, student-generated assessment seems to be gaining interest and exposure thanks to Robert Marzano's work on the 'art and science of teaching' (Marzano 2007; 2017). Marzano identifies three types of assessment used in our schools: obtrusive, unobtrusive and student-generated. Obtrusive assessments are those we are most used to – they are an 'event' that interrupts the school day, or have a set time that the assessment is due. Unobtrusive assessment does not interfere with the regular day and is performed by the teacher with minimal interruption to students. Student-generated assessment is where students are a part of the creation of the assessment; they determine how they will be assessed, rather than having assessment done *to* them.

The benefits of running student-generated assessment, include:

- meeting students where they are at
- helping students understand what is expected of them
- empowering students to take ownership of their learning and assessment
- motivating students to choose an appropriate level of challenge
- giving choice as to the way in which students demonstrate their knowledge and understanding
- deepening learning, meaning students are more likely to be able to apply the learning to different contexts
- increasing engagement in the task.

In my first year as a full-time data storyteller I worked with a secondary school that trialled student-generated assessment in a range of subject areas and year levels across the school. It was so successful that the school decided to step up the expectation in the following year so that every teacher in every subject ran a student-generated assessment task in at least one term of the year.

A common misconception that I often hear related to student-generated assessment is that it means a different assessment task is set for every student, every time. While that might be one possibility, it is not every teacher's dream to have 25 different versions of each assessment and, let's be honest, it is not practical or realistic. Marzano discusses the notion of proficiency scales and unpacking expectations of student knowledge and understanding with students, so students essentially 'choose' the way they will demonstrate that they are moving up the proficiency scale (Marzano and Brown 2011). This is where there might be the assumption that this will look very different for different students, and that it is a lot more work.

On the contrary: student-generated assessment has the capacity to engage student voice in a smaller number of options, and the assessment options do not have to be unique for each student. For example, student involvement has been used in the construction of exam questions – where students were given topics and levels of difficulty, and asked to develop a bank of questions for the exam. The teacher used the questions generated by the students, put them together in the way that they needed to and developed the overall exam. In another instance, I have seen teachers co-construct extended response essay questions with the class – they wrote four or five questions together, the teacher finalised them, then gave students the questions one week before their 'seen' essay exam. Another option is having a class co-construct three assignment options, and once the three options have been decided on by the class, then each student chooses one to complete.

There is a lot of potential with student-generated assessment; we just need teachers to be willing to try it out. It may not be familiar to you or what you experienced at school, and it may not fit in with the assessment types you learned about at university, but it can have a significant impact on student outcomes.

Deliberate conversations

Of the five modes, deliberate conversation is the one requiring least discussion and explanation – we do this all day, every day! Although there is a range of opportunities for data-informed conversations with students, classes and cohorts, individual conversations can be some of the most specific and targeted, meaning they have greatest impact. They are also, arguably, the mode that we use most frequently, as we are always in conversation with students.

Informal conversations happen regularly with students, whether it be on the quality of work, level of understanding, learner dispositions or navigating social relationships or behaviour.

For the purpose of this book, we will focus on formal conversations that use data and evidence to start or guide the conversation. These conversations might be less frequent, but have the potential to provide students with useful information about their performance, and tangible ways to move forward.

Data on walls in classrooms

The data walls discussed in Lyn Sharratt and Michael Fullan's work (2012) relate predominantly to the processing, visualisation and storytelling that is done by teachers on data walls; most of which students do not have access to. There is, however, another type of data wall that is more visible to students: student data on walls in classrooms.

My use of the term 'data' here is not limited only to quantitative scores, but includes qualitative data – particularly categorical results or exemplars of student work. Qualitative categorical results are commonly used in schools. Technically they fall into the realm of qualitative data – even though, sometimes, the categories are numbered or have a particular order; and even though, sometimes, grades are equated to numerical values for averaging, visualising or tracking results. Although it may come as a surprise to know, grades (such as A–E) are qualitative data, as the grade result reflects how the quality of student work matches the descriptors in the criteria. The result itself says more about the student work than the letter alone indicates – but only if we (and students) read the descriptors in the rubric. This type of qualitative data is sometimes referred to as ordinal data, as there is an order or hierarchy to the groups; for example, A is higher than B, which is higher than C. This is different to qualitative nominal data, where the categories do not have a hierarchy or order.

The use of data on classroom walls and with students has occurred for decades. The very first data wall that I remember was in my classroom when I was in Year 1. It showed who could and could not tie their shoelaces (more on that in part 3). Also in Year 1, there was a star chart on the wall, with all of our names in alphabetical order. Whenever we earned a star sticker for doing something well, we got to place the star beside our name and see our collection increasing (like a positive behaviour wall). When we reached 10, 20 and 30 stars, we were able to choose a prize from the prize box. It was very clear to see who was 'winning', who had the least amount of stars and where I fit into the group (FYI: I never 'won' – I always had way too much to say!).

Many of my primary school teachers also showcased examples of student work on classroom walls. There were writing examples, mathematical working and pieces of artwork. While some teachers put everyone's art on a string hanging across the room, some only put the best examples; and when we did a similar task in the future, students were directed to go and look at the example of work to get an idea of how to improve.

Examples such as these, as well as many others, exist in many classrooms today. Sometimes the data on walls might be related to an important skill that students are trying to achieve (such as the shoelace example), but they can also be used to categorise student behaviour, showcase the best work samples, show completed competencies, rank students or show proficiency at different levels.

The benefits of having this information on classroom walls are largely related to the power of visualisations, providing exemplars and the comparison with peers. By visualising information and results to students in this way, we tap into the inherent power of visual representations, which are far superior to any other type of information we have access to. Research tells us that it can take as little as 13 milliseconds to process an image, we remember up to about 80 per cent of what we see, and up to 90 per cent of all the information that our brains process comes from visualisations (Brown 2018; Einsberg 2014; iDashboards UK 2018). Berger (1972) believes that this is because 'seeing comes before words. The child looks and recognises before it can speak'.

The second reason that having data on walls in classrooms is beneficial is because the learning and achievement becomes more visible to students. Showing samples of student work or exemplars on the walls can help provide clarity about what is expected from students (see Monash University 2023). It can provide detail to a student about how they can improve their work or what is expected of them. Some research indicates that exemplars can help improve student results and achievement. While there are some important considerations to be aware of (see Monash University 2023), they can be incredibly beneficial for the learning process.

The additional benefit that data on classroom walls can provide relates to the notion of comparison among peers. Susan Brookhart (2011; 2017) identifies three types of comparisons that we make in feedback to students: we compare their work to a criterion, to their previous result or performance, or to their peers' work. While my professional experience (and doctoral research) indicates that teachers have mixed views on the notion of competition, comparison and students knowing one another's data, I would argue that comparison is a more widespread practice than we may think. Whether you agree with it or not, I, and countless others, have first-hand experience of this approach working – on the condition that it is done well, and in a way that is supportive, not competitive.

Ultimately, the details of what these classroom walls look like differ considerably. This is largely dependent on the teacher's preferences, student readiness, age and stage of the learners and classroom climate. However, the underlying purpose is to highlight where students are at; and the more often the data is used and engaged with, the more effective it can be. If data is put on classroom walls but not regularly discussed, referred to or altered, it does not have an impact on teaching and learning. What we do know, however, is that when it is used well, it can be a powerful tool to aid and assist learning.

The previous two chapters have considered the why and how of using data with students, but it is important to consider the way we prepare and engage with this process with students. We must set up the necessary conditions for students to ensure data is supportive and helpful for them and their learning.

Chapter 4

Having conversations with students

Now that we have unpacked the reasons why we might use data with students and the modes by which we can do so, it is time to turn our attention to how we involve students in this process to build data-informed learners. Rather than merely viewing this from a theoretical perspective, it is vital that we think about the practicalities and realities of this. After all, there are constructive and not-so-constructive ways to have these conversations. We do not want to go to the effort of preparing and organising the data to have it fall flat because our delivery is not as good as it could be.

Regardless of why and how you do it, the most important element of developing data-informed learners is where you introduce and explain the process to students. Many teacher concerns about using data with students and talking to them about their data relate to potential disappointment, comparison, negativity unexpected reactions. While we must be cognisant of these factors, these issues can be minimised and reduced if teachers and school leaders actively build a culture of psychological safety in classrooms and (more broadly) across the school.

Let's take a look at a few of the concerns that I often hear, and what I think and say in response.

Concern #1: What if the student is disappointed with their progress (in a formative task or activity)?

This conversation differs depending on whether it is related solely to a formative task or activity that does not contribute to a student's overall grade, or a summative task or piece of assessment. If it's for a formative task, my response to this concern would be to ask, 'Isn't it better for students to be disappointed with their progress while they can still do something about it, rather than waiting until the summative assessment?'. Yes, some students will inevitably be disappointed at different times; but it is important that we work with them to help them learn how to manage this disappointment. It's far better to talk to them about how they can make improvements, rather than not talk to them at all, or to wait until it is too late for them to improve.

We know about the power of feedback and the impact that it can have on student achievement. This is an example of where student disappointment can lead to an important formative conversation about their work ethic, approach or application – one that can be transformative in improving a student's understanding of where they are at and what they need to do to improve.

Concern #2: What if the summative assessment result is low or disappointing, and the student or parent/guardian asks what the teacher (or school) is doing to help the student improve?

I understand why this is a concern for teachers, particularly when online data dashboards are rolled out; however, this reflection shifts the conversation and responsibility away from the student being the agent of change onto the teacher. If this situation occurred with a student, parent or guardian, I would recommend discussing steps that the student could take to improve; offering to continue to support the student; reminding the student that, ultimately, change is dependent on them and their decisions; and helping the student plan out a pathway forward. If the comment comes directly from the parent or guardian after the conversation with the student, explain the discussion that you had with the student, including possible steps they could take to improve, and that you will continue to support them. Remember, students are the agents of change here; ultimately, they need to take responsibility for their achievement. If you're able to frame this as building the student's self-regulation, independence or ownership of learning, embrace the opportunity to do so.

On some occasions, there may be structural or logistical changes that are required and made as a result of low performance (for example, shifting the student's seating position in the classroom, changing classes or adjusting assessment). In this case, ensure that you discuss these options with the student and their parent/guardian, but remember to keep returning the conversation to the student owning their achievement and choices. These changes are made with the goal of benefiting the student, but the student still needs to take the opportunity to learn in a different way, mode or context.

More often than not, I have seen parents and guardians express appreciation for the availability of the information in a different format; thank the school for the work they're doing to embed learning analytics; and even (cheekily) ask how they can get even more information about how their child is going!

Concern #3: What if using data in conversations with students builds competition between them?

While I have not personally seen this unfold negatively, I understand that, if handled incorrectly, it is possible that conversations with students about data could potentially lead to negative competitive interactions between students. They are kids, after all. However, I also know that this is rare, and if the conversation and information-sharing is well-managed by the teacher, negative reactions can be prevented.

There are a couple of factors that are worth thinking about to begin with. Don't share a student's data with their peers unless they have granted permission; if you do want to talk broadly about class performance, use averages and de-identified data where possible (or seek permission from every student in the class before sharing class results). These are generally common-sense rules, but it is important to mention them here. Gone are the days where teachers would call out names and grades publicly to the class; however, I did meet a teacher a few years ago who still returned student assessments to the class from highest to lowest performer, and didn't think it was a problem because he didn't read out the results! Ultimately, we need to be sensitive to these challenges, and we can deal with them. Later in this chapter I offer a list of dos and don'ts for having data conversations with students – check out that list before you get started.

Concern #4: Data is private, and students shouldn't know other students' results

While I don't advocate for the approach I experienced in the United Kingdom, where all Year 9 Science students were ranked from top to bottom in the main corridor, I believe that we can think outside the box a little bit when it comes to discussing data with students. I've worked with students in a range of different contexts, and found that transparency with student results, when handled delicately and respectfully, can lead to rich conversations with students and among students.

A quote that I regularly come back to when talking about working with numbers is from Charles Seife, who stated, in his book *Proofiness: How You're Being Fooled by the Numbers* (2010):

> *For a non-mathematician, numbers are interesting only when they give us information about the world. A number only takes on any significance in everyday life when it tells us how many pounds we've gained since last month or how many dollars it will cost to buy a sandwich or how many weeks are left before our taxes are due.*

In the context of using student data with students, this quote reminds us that allowing students to put a context around their results is just as important as that context is for us as their teachers. Telling a student their grade, but not telling them their position in the class or cohort, or how they went compared to the student they work with, makes it difficult for students to understand their performance. Showing exemplars of student work that meet higher-level descriptors helps students understand where they are at and what they need to do to improve. It is the context around the data that helps students make sense of what it means.

In every instance where I have showed de-identified data to a class (and only the individual students knew which data belonged to them), students very quickly started talking to one another and told others where they sat. Because the results ended up being well known, shared and discussed in the classroom anyway, we ended up re-identifying the data so it was easier to track. I have no doubt that the way in which I spoke with students about their information, our collective strengths and gaps and the importance of working together as a team contributed to them being open and willing to discuss their results with others. They did not see it as a competition or a hierarchy; it was us, together, trying to do the best we could.

As the adult in the room, we know that student results are point-in-time, they are not perfect and they do not measure or track everything we know about a student – including what type of human they are, how hard they worked or the huge number of skills they have in other areas. Have this conversation with students and trust that they will recognise that some people do better at different times and at different things, but it is all about the group improving together. Different students will excel in different subjects and activities at different times. Normalise the fact that we all have unique strengths, and students will start to see that it is not a competition or a negative exercise.

Concern #5: My students aren't used to talking about their data, so they won't be able to engage effectively

Like any skill that we learn throughout our lifetime, students will need to be taught how to talk about their data and how to have respectful conversations with their peers about their progress. If your students have never been given a chance to reflect on their data or have discussions about their current level of work, what they are working on improving and what they need to do next, they probably will find this tricky the first time they do this.

Start slowly and provide support and scaffolding to help them have the conversation. Think about the three elements I discussed in part 1 – data literacy, data visualisation and data storytelling – and deliberately step students through each of these. Build their understanding of the numbers or data – ensure they know what it means and what information you are providing to them. Make sure they know what is 'good', 'average' and 'low', to give them some context around the data so it makes sense to them. Next, unpack the different ways you have visualised the information. Ensure students know how to read and interpret the visualisations that show their data.

When you get to data storytelling, think about the following two questions and how you might support students to ask them and reflect on them:

1. What insights are there in the data?
2. What do we do about those insights?

Support students to build their skills in identifying the insights, then think about the questions you could ask to engage them in a conversation about their learning. In addition, there is a list of dos and don'ts later in this chapter – take a read of these and think about them before you embark on this new approach. It might be daunting at first, but you, and your students, will become more comfortable with this process as you practise.

Levels of student involvement and teacher skill

In their book *Leaders of Their Own Learning: Transforming Schools Through Student-Engaged Assessment*, Berger et al. (2014) discuss the ways in which teachers can have conversations with students about their data. They categorise the skill of teachers having data conversations as either beginning, intermediate or advanced stages. According to the authors, beginning is where:

> *School leaders and teachers collect and analyse student achievement data as well as data on progress toward state and Common Core standards, habits of work, and student engagement. Often a robust faculty practice of data collection and analysis leads to bringing data practices into the classroom to use with students.*

It is interesting to note that the authors reference both achievement and progress in their description of the beginning level. At this point it is important to remember that achievement data is the overall grade – the number of As in a test, for example. This collection of data is usually the most common in classrooms, because they are what must happen. Progress measures, on the other hand, are not compulsory in reporting to parents; they are optional. However, data on progress potentially has more impact on student learning and motivation than just an achievement grade at the end of a unit. According to Berger et al. (2014), both types of data must be collected on students and both appear at this beginning level.

Another element of this description that is of interest is the statement that there is 'often a robust faculty practice of data collection and analysis [which] leads to bringing data practices into the classroom'. Having a robust practice of data collection and analysis is an important first step, because it is through the expectations of the department leader and colleagues and the data conversations within these teams that teachers learn the language of data and the questions to ask. Like all elements of our practice, learning how to use data takes time; it makes sense that the more we are exposed to talking about data with colleagues in a safe space – where we can ask questions, learn from others and occasionally get it wrong – the more we build our confidence and willingness to have data conversations with students. The challenge is that, if a teacher is not part of a faculty or teaching team that regularly has these discussions, they may not be confident in their own ability to talk about the data, and thus even more apprehensive about their ability to get it right with students.

Following this discussion, Berger et al. (2014) identify characteristics of educators and students working at this level. These characteristics are as follows:

- *Teachers set up a data-safe classroom culture in which students have a growth mindset. They strive to personally improve, but don't compete against each other.*

- *Students learn the language of data.*

- *Teachers build student confidence using data, giving them early wins with skills or behaviours that they can measure and improve. Often this is a collective effort.*

- *Teachers establish a system for collecting student work (e.g., in work folders).*

The final points of the 'beginning teacher' description relate to the culture and climate that the teacher builds. I truly believe that students value what we value. Whether it's pride in their work, completion of homework, working well with others or using data in the classroom, students build their confidence in our approaches based on our belief and passion. For example, if a teacher went into a classroom and began the data conversation activity by saying something like the following, the buy-in from students would not be as good as it could have been:

Okay students, all your teachers have to have conversations with you about how you're tracking this year. Let's just get it done as quickly as we can so we can get back to our other work.

Alternatively, if a teacher started with something like the following, this is much more likely to engage students and help them see that the process is beneficial and should be taken seriously:

Over the next few lessons I'll be sitting down with each of you to talk about your goals and progress in this subject. Having conversations about where we're tracking is really useful because it helps you understand where you're at, and we can then discuss how you can improve and set some goals to work on together.

In addition, explaining that we'd like them to take the process seriously, and calling students out on any disengagement in the process, is an important next part of the journey.

The second level of Berger et al.'s (2014) use of data with students is when teachers move to the intermediate level. Intermediate-level teachers are those who:

use a data-inquiry cycle to ensure that students are meeting state and Common Core standards. They continually assess student progress and adjust instruction. Students are included and involved in understanding their data and setting goals.

I appreciate the reference in this description to inquiry cycles and regularly assessing student progress. This speaks to what I often see when I'm working with highly effective practitioners in using data – data is not an event, or something they only do at set meetings with set outcomes. It is who they are, and it is inherently part of their day-to-day. Berger et al. (2014) describe intermediate users as follows:

- *Teachers develop tools, such as learning target trackers or error analysis forms, to assist students in collecting data. Whenever appropriate students are taught to use digital tools for data collection.*

- *Teachers and students share the responsibility for identifying what data to gather and analyse. A strong culture of safety and collaboration is in evidence.*

- *Results of data analysis not only support student pride and strength but also highlight areas of need that provide opportunities for reflection and goal setting.*

- *Students set goals based on individual or group work and have an established system and routine in place to track their progress. Students have access to the data about their progress.*

- *Student work folders or portfolios are dynamic classroom tools, used regularly to help students track their progress.*

- *Teachers and students mutually decide how and when to report data and growth to families, often during student-led conferences or passage presentations.*

It becomes clear, through these descriptors, that at an intermediate level students become key partners in this process. There are routines and processes in place – relating to the types of data used, analysis, goal setting and tracking – and students understand their role in these processes. In addition, the use of data in this way and at this level has a clear impact on students' pride in and understanding of themselves as learners. It is, authentically, a shared responsibility and engagement in the process.

The final level of Berger et al.'s (2014) stages of using data with students is the advanced level, which is described as follows:

- *A comprehensive portfolio system enables students to house data about their progress and tell the story of their learning.*
- *Students are responsible for their own data analysis and share their findings with their teacher(s) and family.*
- *Student goals are specific and individual.*
- *Students are comfortable with and are expected to maintain their own work folders, portfolios, or digital data-collection systems.*
- *Data analysis is a daily or weekly routine.*
- *Students' goals and action plans are written independently and critiqued by teachers.*
- *Students prepare data analysis and visualisations for an audience beyond themselves and their teacher (e.g., at passage presentations).*

This, in all honesty, might appear to be a high aspiration of data use with students, but I would argue that it is possible if there is a concerted effort to engage students in the process and build their capacity. At this level, there are significantly greater expectations on the students themselves and the teachers are facilitators of the process.

In my Physical Education classroom in the United Kingdom, I saw my Year 11 students working at this level. They were tracking their own performance, they were setting goals and regularly reviewing them and they were using predictions and anticipated results to guide their work and focus. The fact that they had to be able to explain to Ofsted inspectors and school leaders running lesson observations what their target grade was, what level they were currently working at and what they needed to do to improve and achieve their target grade undoubtedly contributed to students' understanding of their data.

In a primary school context, I saw this most profoundly when I visited a Northern Territory Learning Commission (NTLC) day in 2022, where students presented their projects from the year. Students from Alawa Primary School, under the guidance of their Principal, Sandy Cartwright, talked me through their use of data and the data portfolios that they had created. All students had their own personalised portfolio of their data, including summative assessment results, standardised testing reports and visualisations, report cards, goal setting information and external academic competition data. The students who presented this approach talked me through the different data, what the different visualisations meant and how they could be interpreted, and they discussed ways students might use the information to inform their goals. At the time, I joked that they were putting me out of work; but I also reflected on the impact not only of students knowing themselves as learners in this way, but the incredibly data-literate young people that will be coming through the ranks if we provide opportunities such as these. Figure 2 shows a poster created by students at the school.

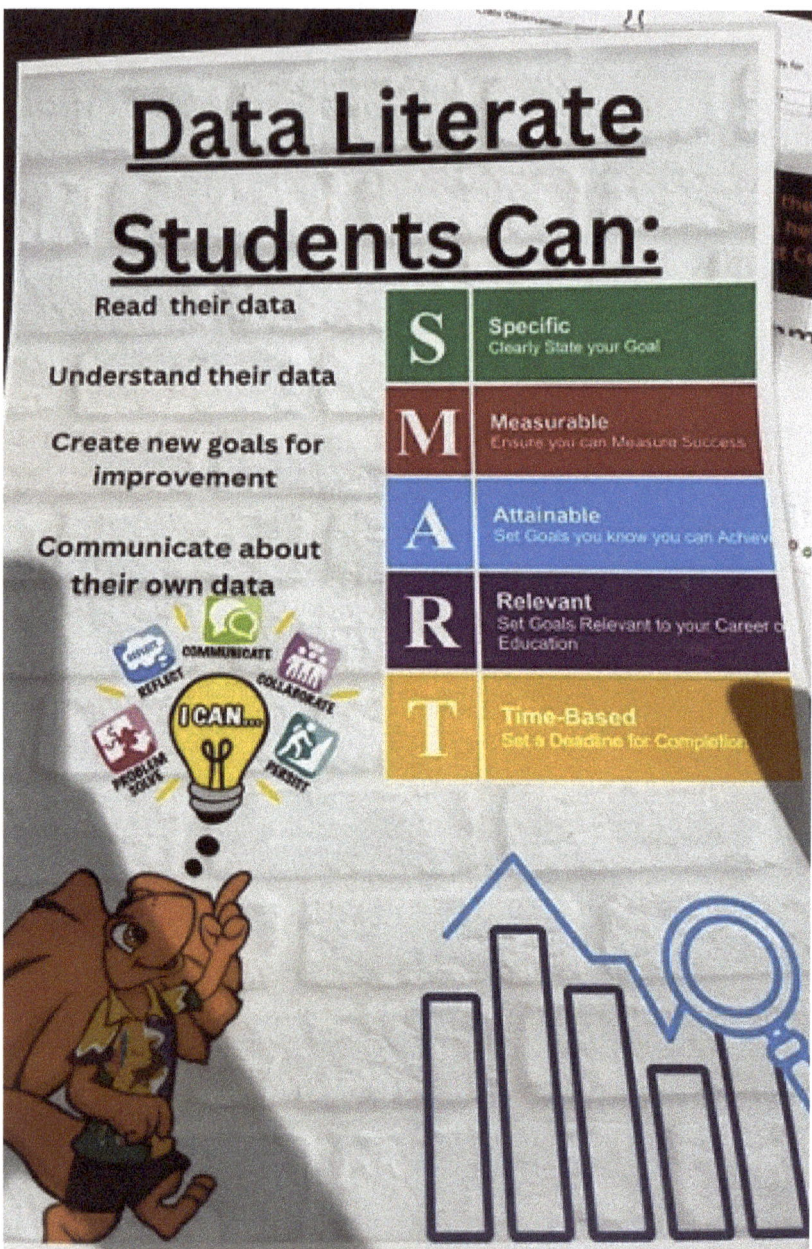

Figure 2: Poster created by students at Alawa Primary School and presented at the NTLC

The purpose of sharing these examples with you, along with the work of Berger et al. (2014), is to get you thinking about where you are positioned in your use of data with students. Do you most closely align with the 'beginner' level? Or are you in the 'intermediate' or 'advanced' stage? What might have been mentioned in the descriptions of these levels that got you thinking? Regardless of where you are at on your journey with engaging students in their data story, there are always ideas and different options available.

Tips for the conversation

When you are embarking on data conversations with students there are a few things to be mindful of, both before and during the conversation. Berger et al. (2014) state that one of the common challenges to using data with students is 'neglecting to build a safe, skilful environment', so we need to makes sure we do this. While having conversations about data with students might be relatively new to you, it is worth remembering that you talk to students all the time – so in that respect, it is not too different to doing what you are very comfortable and natural at. We are just adding more tangible evidence.

Table 3 (overleaf) outlines some important dos and don'ts for having these conversations with students. Remember, when we frame the conversation as being one that is designed to support the learner and help them achieve their goals, it is easier for us to lean into.

The list of dos and don'ts provides some tips as to how you can (and shouldn't) approach these conversations. I encourage you to look through the list and think about what you might already be doing, and some of the things that you could work on next.

Table 3: Dos and don'ts for having data conversations with students

Dos	Don'ts
Before the conversation	
- Explain *why* students will benefit from the conversation about their data. - Show students that you genuinely believe in the benefits of the data-informed conversation. - Acknowledge the limitations of the data – talk about what information it does and does not provide. - Recognise students differ in skills, progress, and achievement – that is completely okay and normal. - Acknowledge potential discomfort – sometimes there will be data that you are not happy with, but there are always opportunities to learn and improve. - Build students' data literacy – ensure they understand the types of data you will be using, what it means, and what is 'good', 'average' and 'low'. - Build students' data visualisation skills – ensure they can read and interpret the visualisations and identify trends.	- Don't imply that the conversation is something that has to be done for compliance. - Don't project negativity about the process – remember, students value what we value. - Don't single out individual students to highlight examples (unless you de-identify the data and are certain that it is not obvious who it belongs to). - Don't show all student data to all students (without individual prior conversations, and/or without de-identifying it). - Don't assume students have good data literacy, visualisation or storytelling skills. - Don't expect students to be able to do all of this well the first time.
During the conversation	
- Start slowly. - Include multiple data sources and talk about trends across triangulated information. - Use values and digits that students can understand (where possible, use single digits – see Heath and Starr 2022). - Encourage students to lead the conversation. - Focus on the data storytelling – ask them to unpack what they see and what it means for them. - Focus on the learning behaviours that lead to improvement in results. - Detail goals and aspirations that have specific and achievable action points and next steps.	- Don't go too fast. - Don't focus on summative assessment grades only (remember to triangulate across multiple data sets). - Don't use abstract numbers that students struggle to understand (for example, very large or very small numbers – see Heath and Starr 2022). - Don't dominate the conversation. - Don't tell students what they should be able to see or what they need to do. - Don't set goals that are of a similar ilk to 'get a B+ in maths this semester' (be specific about what they are aiming to achieve). - Don't allow students to set vague and broad goals without measurable process steps.

This brings us to a close of part 2. We have unpacked the purpose and reasons for using data with students, and outlined the modes through which engaging students in their data story might occur. The final chapter of this section also outlined different levels of proficiency with using data with students, and provided some suggested approaches for engaging with this work and building psychological safety in your classroom.

Next, part 3 highlights a range of examples of how using data with students could look in classrooms and schools, and it is the most significant part of this book. This has been done deliberately, so that practical examples make up the majority of this conversation – because ultimately we need to find out what options are available, and what might work for us in our context, and then put them into practice.

PART 3

Data-informed learners in practice

As we discussed in part 2, we might use data with students in relation to goal setting, behaviour or learner dispositions, or the quality of work or learning. The modes by which we can do so include data walls, success criteria, student-generated assessment, conversations, or data on classroom walls. When the why and how are represented in a table (see table 4), there are 15 possible intersections – these are all opportunities for engaging students in their data story.

Table 4: Intersections of purpose and mode for data-informed learners

		Purpose		
		Goal setting	Behaviour or learner dispositions	Quality of learning
Mode	Data walls	A	F	K
	Success criteria	B	G	L
	Student-generated assessment	C	H	M
	Deliberate conversations	D	I	N
	Data on walls	E	J	O

The examples in part 3 step through these 15 intersections, providing specific ways that you can potentially use different modes to achieve different outcomes. Because some of these approaches are more relevant and are therefore used more frequently in the classroom, you'll find a different number of examples for each intersection. Regardless, the examples chosen are some of the best examples of the ways in which you could approach this in your classroom or school.

Like all of my books, the examples provided here are not exhaustive, and they will not all apply to each teacher, student or school in the same way. They are, however, designed to get you thinking about the possibilities and potential options for your practice. We know that context matters in schools, and it is up to you to ascertain how you could use some of these ideas in a way that suits your circumstances. I encourage you to use the examples as prompts and adapt the ideas so that they work for you, in the best way possible.

The examples provide a mix of both progress and achievement data. While progress is not represented in all the intersections (in fact, there are many more achievement examples than progress), there are countless opportunities to use both types of data in your classroom. Again, I encourage you to identify what works for you – if the example is for achievement data but you think of a way to represent progress data, do that. Or if the example is for progress data and you want to flip it to achievement data, go for it.

You know your students better than anyone – use these examples in whatever way best suits them.

Chapter 5

Intersection A: Goal setting and data walls

The first intersection that we are going to look at is goal setting and data walls. This intersection is a tricky place to start, as in most instances, data walls are developed for use by teachers only. However, there are examples of where they can be used with and for students, helping them understand their performance and set goals.

Teachers setting goals from the data wall

One use, which is aligned with the original intention of data walls, is that teachers use the information on the wall (and the position of their students) to generate ideas about goals that they could work with students on. For example, if your data wall shows progress and achievement in writing samples, you might look at the position of each student in your class, and use this information to guide a conversation with them about what their next writing goal might be.

In one of my previous schools, we had a data wall that represented overall achievement in senior Physical Education, which sat in the Head of Department's office (see figure 3). Two classes were represented on the same data wall. As teachers, we discussed our students' positions and what we could do to help them improve their results. At the class level, we discussed and celebrated some of the hugely positive movements on the wall, and engaged in data storytelling and goal setting with the whole class. As we talked about this more frequently, students asked to see where they sat; so we invited them in to see their position on the wall, and spoke to them specifically about how they were tracking.

Although the movement depicted in figure 3 might seem extreme at the highest and lowest ends, the data wall, at the point of the photo being taken, shows the difference between the end of a formative year, compared with 10 weeks into the summative year. Given that Physical Education in this jurisdiction at the time was 50 per cent theoretical and 50 per cent practical, student results at the beginning of the year were quite heavily skewed by their ability in the first sport that was assessed. This is an important part of the context, and featured significantly in the conversations with students. For some students this was their strongest sport, and for others it was their weakest sport, but either way, it was an important part of the conversation.

Student engagement with data walls

In a school that I used to work in, we had a data wall in a staffroom corridor that triangulated student results for literacy. It was positioned outside the Deputy Principal's office, meaning that students could not see the data wall easily – only on a rare occasion. Student data cards were positioned on the wall based on their progress and achievement in a writing assessment. Left to right showed their achievement (on a 0–24 scale); the vertical height demonstrated growth (top), the same result (middle) or a lower result (bottom). This view enabled teachers to see the number of students who had improved. Different year levels had different-coloured cards so we could see how different year levels were performing. We could also see the number of students below the goal of 20 (out of 24).

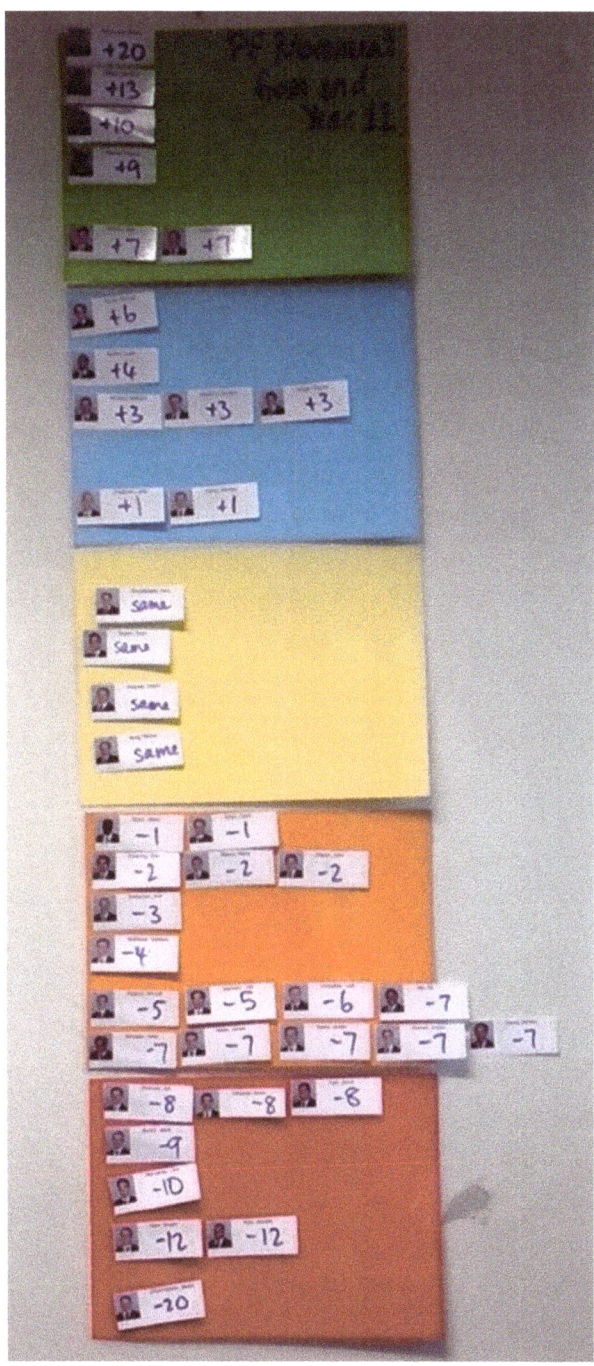

Figure 3: Data wall showing student achievement in senior Physical Education

In addition, when they looked at a specific data card, teachers could see how the writing result aligned (or didn't) with other literacy assessments that the student had completed.

After one series of assessments, it was clear that some Year 9 students significantly underperformed in the writing task – largely due to disengagement and poor behaviour, not because of their ability or skill. The Principal was not happy with the results, so he brought some of the students into the corridor to talk to them about their position on the data wall. The Principal and the students had a conversation about where they felt they should be. The Principal indicated that he thought they could do much better than what they had, and they spoke about engagement and effort. The conversation concluded with students saying that they would try harder next time as they were not happy with where they were positioned, and they could see that it was not good enough. While it might not be the traditional use of a data wall, it actually did lead to improvement the following time, as students could see evidence of the impact of their behaviour.

Goal setting using online data visualisation dashboards

Online data dashboards provide an alternative option to physical data walls. In my work as a data storyteller, I've seen the great impact that data visualisation dashboards can have on teachers and their teaching practice. Increasingly, schools are also using these tools with students and parents/guardians, and providing independent access to summaries of student results. For some schools, these dashboards are now the go-to place for updates to student results and achievement; and they are often updated continuously, with formative and summative assessment.

I've worked with a number of schools that have rolled out these dashboards to staff in the first instance, and have then provided access to parents/guardians and students over time. While this requires planning around the rollout and implementation with these key groups, it is a key strategy in engaging students with their data and helping them take ownership of their results – both at a point in time, as well as longitudinally throughout their educational career.

In my nephew Jhye's final year of secondary school I was involved in goal-setting conversations using dashboards, with his mentor Andrew. We had the opportunity to schedule a short meeting with Andrew during parent-teacher interviews to discuss Jhye's performance and trends across subjects.

In the meeting, Andrew showed a summary of Jhye's performance across different subject areas (as shown in figures 4 and 5). We looked at his attendance, and his performance in different internal assessments, across his six subjects. We could view his GPA over time, as well as seeing trends in each of his subjects. During the meeting, Andrew acknowledged the improvements that Jhye had made, and had a conversation with him about his goals for the next 12 months.

Without access to this visualisation dashboard, this conversation would not have been as easy as it was. If we didn't have access to the dashboard, we would have had to manually view each assessment task individually in the learning management system. As there was no central spot for visualising longitudinal information in the learning management system, we would have had to do a lot more thinking about what the trends were, as we navigated around a different page for each assessment task in each subject area. In contrast, the dashboard allowed us to see this information all in one place, and made comparisons very easy. Consequently,

Data-Informed Learners

the goal-setting conversation focused on Jhye and what he was going to do next, rather than us spending time trying to ascertain patterns and insights.

Figure 4: Dashboard used during mentoring conversation showing semester results and GPA

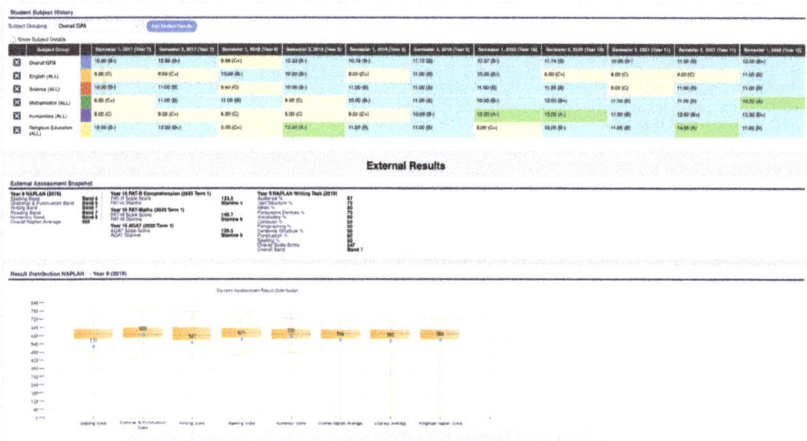

Figure 5: Dashboard used during mentoring conversation showing longitudinal trend and standardised testing results

Chapter 6

Intersection B: Goal setting and success criteria

The second intersection is when we use success criteria to help students set goals. As mentioned in part 2, this is particularly powerful when success criteria are co-constructed with students, but this does not always have to be the case; instead, teachers might construct the success criteria themselves, share them with students and unpack them in the classroom. Co-construction of success criteria is not a process that you would use all the time, or in every lesson; however, if there are times where students work on a topic or skill over time, it can be a powerful approach.

Co-constructed success criteria on a classroom wall

In my work in schools, I have seen numerous examples of teachers using co-constructed success criteria with students to help them set goals. These success criteria are often displayed on classroom walls if they represent a significant learning intention or element of learning in the curriculum or unit.

One example that I first heard about from Lyn Sharratt but have seen a few times in practice is the co-construction of success criteria for writing a sentence. We spoke about this in detail in part 2. As sentence-writing is a skill that takes time to master, it makes sense that co-constructing success criteria could be a good use of time. The criteria can continue to be used for a number of weeks at a time, and they help students unpack what is expected of them.

The co-constructed success criteria can be posted on the classroom wall. Students can then self-reflect and, in conversation with the teacher, establish what they did well and what their next goal is. They can then reflect this on a data wall. One way I have seen this done is where students place a sticky note with their name (or a data card) beside the element of 'writing a sentence' that they are focusing on at that point in time – for example, ensuring the sentence makes sense when it is read out loud. If and when their focus changes, students can move their sticky note or data card to the next element. Alternatively, students can write their name under each of the success criteria once they feel they have achieved the descriptor. As they work on the skill and develop over time, they progressively add their name to each of the descriptors, with the goal of being able to do all the things listed in the success criteria. This could be done with a page under the success criteria where students write their name (either plain paper, or laminated so they can use whiteboard markers), or by providing a list of all student names under each success criteria so students can tick their name off when they feel they can demonstrate the skill.

Co-constructed success criteria in student books

An additional iteration of the co-constructed success criteria shown in the previous example is to make the student engagement in the process less public. For example, instead of putting the criteria on the wall the teacher can print a checklist or goal-setting template for students to stick into their books to complete (as shown in figure 6). This example would allow students to tick or colour in each star when they feel they can do each element.

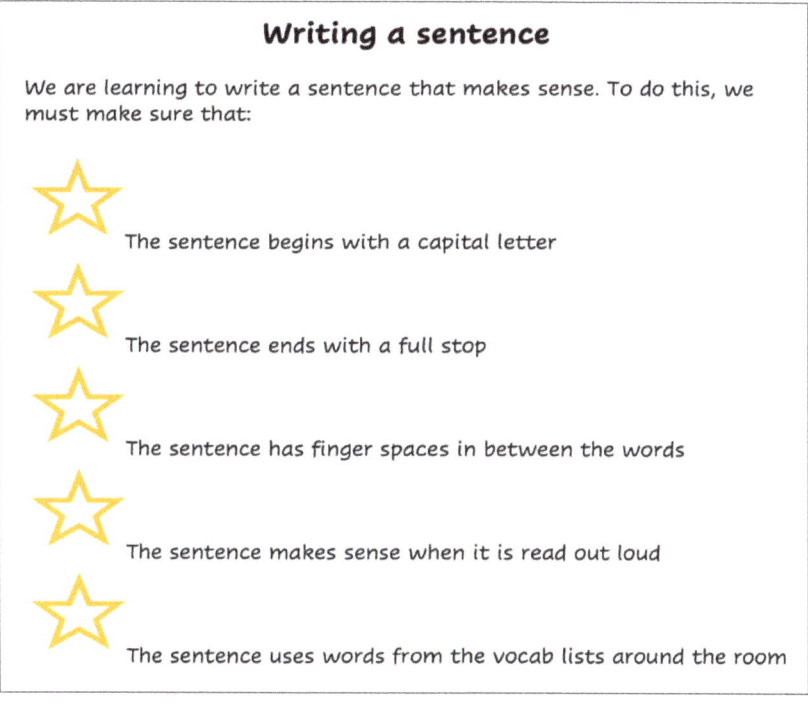

Figure 6: Example of a printed success-criteria template that is stuck in a student's book

For older students, it is also possible to have an electronic version for them to store in their online/electronic workbooks. In the same way as the hard-copy example, students could change the colour or place a tick mark beside each of the descriptors as they are able to demonstrate the skill.

Bump it up walls

Another way of helping students set goals through clear indications of what success looks like is with a bump it up wall. Lyn Sharratt (2019) says that bump it up walls have the capacity to:

show students that through self-assessment:

- *learning is iterative*
- *it gets better with feedback and successive attempts*
- *improvement is possible*
- *work can always get better, and*
- *students look for ways to improve and never settle for the first attempt.*

Bump it up walls demonstrate different levels of student responses. They are useful because they allow students to identify characteristics on the wall that align with their own work, and see an example of work that is at a higher level than theirs so that they have something to aim for.

While bump it up walls do not necessarily need to relate to grades, they should contain roughly four to six levels of work that increasingly demonstrate success in the task, or different levels of skill. A common recommendation is that the lowest level on the wall should always be below the lowest student's ability in the class, so no one is on the lowest level. Similarly, students should see a sample that is higher than the highest student in the class. The idea is that all students are provided with an example of student work that is a stretch for them.

There are plenty of examples of bump it up walls available online. One version available for download from the Teach Starter website (Smith 2020): www.teachstarter.com/au/blog/narrative-writing-examples-bump-it-up-wall/. See also figure 7.

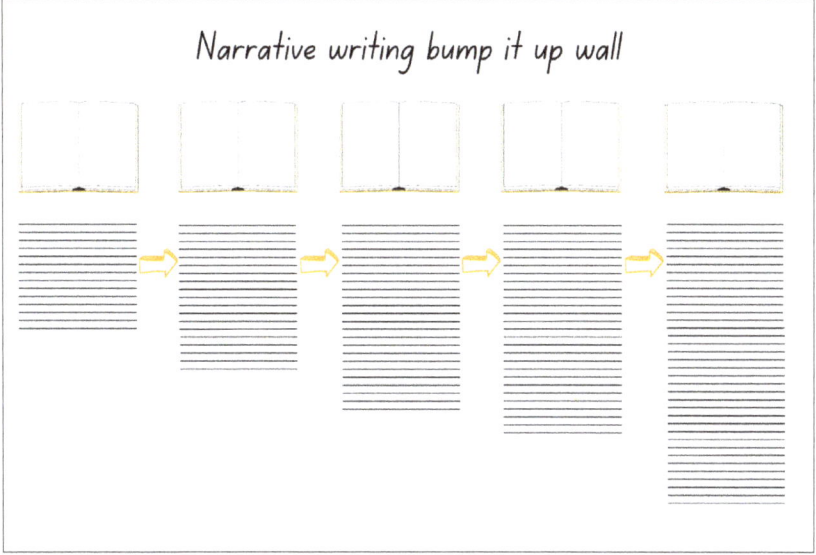

Figure 7: A sample bump it up wall

There are a few ways teachers can engage students in goal setting using bump it up walls. Students could have a card with their name on it that they place on the level that they believe they are working at. As students seek to improve their work they can move their card as they experience success. Another option is for students to put an annotated note on the level they are aiming for, potentially also identifying their main focus or aim that will help them 'level up'.

If you or your students would prefer a more private version of this, they could have a reflection page in their workbook (or online notebook) where they reflect on the current level they are on, why they believe they are positioned at that level, and what they need to do to bump up to the next level. You could enhance this process by providing samples of the aspiration level to students with annotated comments, and have them identify the things they feel they can do, and the things they are working on.

Either way, bump it up walls provide students an opportunity to see what success looks like and set goals about improving their work so they can move to the next level. By seeing exemplars of student work at different levels, students can identify their skills and level of achievement, and set targeted and specific goals about what they need to do to improve.

Chapter 7

Intersection C: Goal setting and student-generated assessment

The third intersection gets us thinking about goal setting and student-generated assessment. Student-generated assessment is a great way to motivate students to engage in conversations about goal setting, and to have them setting their own goals with a strategy for how they will achieve them. Student-generated assessment clearly positions students as agents of change.

Proficiency scales

Robert Marzano's (2007; 2017) proficiency scales, which we looked at in chapter 3, are a good example of students using student-generated assessment to set and achieve goals in their chosen subject area. I have seen a few different variations in the use of proficiency scales in the schools I have visited, but I would like to highlight just one here.

A secondary school that I worked with had proficiency scales for virtually everything, across subject areas and year levels 7 to 10. Like Marzano recommends, the proficiency scales were numbered 0–4, and they outlined and documented student proficiency and ability at each level. It was, and remains, the only school that I have seen that has implemented proficiency scales as rigorously and comprehensively as this.

The great thing about the way the school used the proficiency scales was that, to complement this practice, students had one student-generated assessment task per year in most (if not all) of their subjects. Students were quite used to using proficiency scales and setting goals to move up the levels; however, when teachers introduced the notion of student-generated assessment, it took student agency and motivation to another level.

The school utilised a few different methods of running student-generated assessment – for example, co-constructing seen or unseen exams, and having a handful of student-generated assessment tasks to choose from. The one I would like to highlight here was in Visual Arts, where students were permitted to set goals with the proficiency scale and demonstrate their skill and understanding in whatever way, shape or form they wanted to.

The teacher and students unpacked the levels of the proficiency scale, and the teacher showed (and had available) examples of student work at the different levels of proficiency. The teacher detailed the specific skills, knowledge and understanding that students would need to demonstrate to progress up the levels, and this was a conversation that the teacher came back to multiple times throughout the unit. Students spent time early on in the unit, with the proficiency scale, unpacking the expectations, setting a goal for what they were working towards, then outlining a host of ways that they could (and would) demonstrate their skills.

As the unit progressed, students had opportunities to approach the teacher and demonstrate proficiency in different elements at different levels. If the student achieved their goal, the teacher assessed it, gave feedback, collected it and stored it. However, if the student did not hit their goal, they were given the choice of either going back and working on it again, or accepting the lower level.

The teacher reflected that usually, students would take the initial formative feedback and would go and modify their work and come back to have it reassessed. The teacher also noted that while there were times students were not happy with the result and took the opportunity to modify the work, in most instances, because of their thorough understanding of the proficiency scale, they often achieved the result they were after in their first go. If the teacher felt the student was coasting, or was being a bit conservative with their goals, she challenged them to aim higher by connecting elements of their work with descriptors in the higher level.

Undoubtedly, this required a lot of set-up and time to build student understanding about proficiency scales; but because using data in this way was the norm in their school across subject areas, the extra time and effort was truncated. For the teacher, there was ongoing assessment, review and extensive documentation of where students were at. However, the teacher reported that she felt it was worth the effort, and said that students had achieved some of their best-ever results due to taking charge of their learning and assessment. A brilliant by-product of this task was that students were able to talk specifically about what success looked like, where they were at and what they needed to do to improve. Further, students became resources for one another, as they were able to support each other and discuss skills, successes and attributes of their work with others who wanted to progress. On top of this, the teacher had no marking to do at the end of the unit. It really was a win-win.

Health and Physical Education assignment

A few years ago I ran a webinar on student-generated assessment and the following example was shared with me. Unfortunately I do not remember the name of the teacher who shared it; but I thought it was such a great idea that I couldn't *not* include it here.

The example was an assessment task for a Year 10 Health and Physical Education unit on drug use and smoking. Rather than the assessment task being a regular assignment, as we have come to know and expect, this assessment task was different. It provided students a host of different ways in which to complete the assignment, through gaining a certain number of 'points' in the tasks that they completed. They had to complete a minimum of 10 points successfully to pass the unit.

Some of the tasks that students could complete were relatively low in points value (for example, earning them one, two or three points). These asked students to complete easier and smaller tasks that assessed lower-order thinking, such as recall, identify and explain. As the level of cognitive difficulty increased, students gained more points for these tasks – earning upwards to five, six and seven points. This task was student-generated in that there were around 15 to 20 options for assessment completion; students could choose how they accumulated their 10 points, with some conditions to ensure they covered all the assessment elements.

There were limitations, of course. For example, if students chose all one, two, and three point activities, the maximum grade they could achieve was a C, as these tasks were aligned with that achievement standard. But if they completed one larger task that assessed higher-order skills, and then a couple of smaller tasks, they were potentially able to achieve an A or B grade, depending on the quality of their responses.

I have decided not to replicate the document that this teacher shared on the day here, as I cannot fairly attribute it to the creator; but I hope my explanation of his work, in some way, does it justice. The teacher reported that it was a useful approach, as students had a lot of autonomy in the way they completed their assessment: they had complete choice as to how they earned their 10 points and what that looked like as a final product, all within the parameters of predetermined activities and tasks that were consistent across the year level. I thought it was pretty great!

Science example folio and resubmission of student work to achieve goals

Earlier in my teaching career I was lucky enough to work with a brilliant Head of Science, Kev. Kev was not only innovative and ahead of his time in terms of collaboration, inquiry learning and strategies to engage students, but also great at wearing Hawaiian shirts on Fridays. One of the many things that I learned from Kev was to in relation to middle-school Science. He taught me that not only should we assess students using exams and assignments, but we should also consider the power and utility of folio work. When I was teaching in his department, students in Years 8 to 10 had one term per year where their assessment was a folio only, with no other exams or assignments.

As teachers, we had flexibility in what we included in the folio for students – but there were some parameters, obviously, around needing to ensure that we had evidence of students being able to demonstrate (and work above) the achievement standard, and including both science knowledge and skills in the folio. For me, each term, I planned out seven or eight activities to complete, with one due each week. There were a number of years that I taught Year 9 Science. I would plan out activities such as:

- a practical activity write-up
- completion of questions and solutions to activities

- detailed discussion from an in-class experiment
- science inquiry challenges, which combined science, technology, engineering and mathematics
- activities where students designed or ideated solutions to problems
- reflections on learning, group tasks, collaboration and so on.

Each week, students would need to submit one of the pieces of the folio. I would then mark the work that was completed and add the results to my spreadsheet, which also contained students' previous results and their goals for the subject. Each piece of the folio was given a score, and the student's overall result was 'predicted' in the final column of the spreadsheet, based on the quality of the folio work that they were submitting.

We had a department-wide policy that students were able to resubmit their folio tasks if they were not happy with the result they had achieved. We encouraged them to do so if they were achieving results that meant they were not going to hit their goal. My tracking spreadsheet had this data in it already, so it was an easy comparison for me (and then the students) to make.

I observed that students had a desire to improve, and were often self-motivated to do so. Students felt as though they had more ownership over the tasks and results than they would a single assessment or exam; it was in their power to adjust and improve results if they were not happy with them. Because my spreadsheet predicted grades, I often had students ask me what would happen if they received a specific result in the next task, and they could see that it was equally and fairly weighted. They could make decisions about where and when they would resubmit, invest more time or move on, all relative to the results they were aiming to achieve.

A common question I often faced from teachers in other departments at that school was to do with marking load. There is no doubt that there was more marking required with this approach than marking a single assignment or exam; however, individually, the tasks were not large. There were also were no time limits or deadlines associated with drafting an assignment or preparing an exam, and as long as I stayed on top of the marking each week, it meant that students achieved better results. I also had no marking to complete at the end of term.

Chapter 8

Intersection D: Goal setting and deliberate conversations

Data can be used in deliberate conversations to support progress, goals and achievement, in a range of ways. It largely occurs one-on-one between student and teacher, sometimes with parental involvement. Students and the teacher reflect on the student's progress and achievement; they select future subjects, set goals or talk about the learner dispositions or characteristics that will enable the student to build on their level of skill and understanding and improve in the future. Intersection D is this opportunity, where we have deliberate, often formal, conversations with students about their progress and achievement.

Individual goal setting in the classroom

In my last teaching role I taught a Year 10 Mathematics class. I had taught most of these students for the previous two-and-a-half years. Throughout the extended period of teaching these students, I worked with them on their goals for the subject and got to know them really well as young adults and as learners.

At the beginning of the semester, I would talk with each student individually during class time and we would agree on a grade-based goal for the semester informed by their previous semester result. Going into these conversations, I always put in place a couple of parameters and limitations for the student's goal; for example, if a student was aiming to break into the next grade boundary they had to aim for the lowest result first (so, if they had previously achieved a C+, they could aim for a B-). When they achieved this result we would review it again. During the conversation we talked about the strategies that the student would need to employ throughout the unit to achieve their goals, and we spoke about ways they felt I could help them best.

The first time I ran this activity with a different group of students in Year 11, I asked them what they needed me to do to keep them on track. At the time, many of them said they did very little homework and knew they needed to do more, so they wanted me to regularly track and monitor their homework completion. Consequently, it became a habit for me to track homework completion and formative quiz results rigorously, as practice and fluency are vital to student success in this subject. The interesting thing about the Year 11 students was that they had asked me to keep track, and when I did, they responded well.

For the Year 10 class, I tracked their homework in the same way in a spreadsheet (as shown in figure 8). Each time I checked homework I would colour the cell green, yellow or red (to represent being completed and marked, more than half completed and marked, or less than half completed and marked). Having had the conversation with students prior to this process, and initially de-identifying the spreadsheet, we did get to the point where I could show the tracking spreadsheet on the whiteboard each lesson with all student names and progress. This would occur after I had finished any explicit teaching and group activities, and while students were working on their own.

Name	Attendance	Goal	2A	2B	2C	2D	2E	Revision quiz	6A	6B	6C	6D	6F	6G	6H
Student A	88.9%	B-													
Student B	90.0%	B+													
Student C	74.6%	B-													
Student D	84.1%	D+													
Student E	96.9%	B													
Student F	97.6%	C-													
Student G	90.2%	B													
Student H	91.9%	A-													
Student I	95.1%	A-													
Student J	89.1%	A-													
Student K	89.9%	C+													
Student L	95.9%	A													
Student M	95.5%	C+													
Student N	93.9%	C-													
Student O	85.7%	A-													
Student P	65.8%	B-													
Student Q	90.0%	C-													
Student R	94.5%	A-													
Student S	93.7%	C+													
Student T	89.0%	D+													

Figure 8: Sample spreadsheet tracking for Year 10 Mathematics

Students knew that once the spreadsheet was on the board, they could come to me to update it. Almost every lesson, students would come to me and say things like, 'Miss, I'm a green now for exercise 3A, can I change it?' and they would show me the work, then change the applicable cell on the spreadsheet. Initially, I changed the colours myself and they could see it on the whiteboard; however, students began asking if they could make the changes instead and I let them do it (I could, after all, see what they were doing). It became almost a ritual for them to 'check off' the work they had done, and I could see the sense of accomplishment that they had by doing so.

If students ended up with three red cells, we had an agreement that I would contact home by sending an email to their parents/guardians. Even the most disengaged students did not want me to contact home, so often I would mention to students that they had two red cells prior to setting more homework. I reminded them that they were close to having three, and that they would definitely need to do their homework tonight. Inevitably, they completed the work, I updated the spreadsheet the next day and I rarely had to contact home.

Tracking homework in this way (as well as their results in formative quizzes) enabled me to have ongoing conversations throughout the unit with students about their learning and skill, and progress towards their goal. If students were not completing homework or if they were underperforming on formative tasks, I would touch base with them, reflect on their goals and their distance from them, and discuss what they needed to address if they wanted to achieve their goal. They were good conversations to have as they were completely informed by the evidence at hand.

On the other hand, if students were working well, completing their work and getting formative results that were really pleasing, I found an opportunity to talk to them about this and reflect on their goals. Unsurprisingly there were plenty of pleasing results, and many examples of students achieving a result in a quiz, a section of an exam, or overall results that were their 'best ever'. It was a great opportunity to celebrate growth and achievement, and to smash the assumption that some students believed that they were 'not good at maths'. It was a whole lot of fun proving them wrong.

Scheduled mentoring conversations

At a time when learning analytics data was increasingly available and predictions were being made as to senior students' potential university entrance ranks, I taught in a school that had formalised senior goal-setting conversations with students. These were deliberate, scheduled conversations, informed by data, held between students and a designated mentor teacher. Structured mentoring, particularly of senior students, occurs in many schools, but in this instance, it was coupled with sharing data and visualisations (mostly generated in Microsoft Excel at the time) to assist the process.

Prior to the mentoring meetings, each mentor was provided with a folio of student results – including their results in each of their subject areas, overall predictions, and other effort and behaviour feedback from teachers. At the time, all Year 12 students aiming to go to university sat a core skills test, and they did mock practices throughout the 12-month period preceding the test. Over time, we built visualisations of their performance in the mock exams, so students could see the areas in which they were scoring higher and lower, which ultimately assisted the goal-setting process.

Students worked with their mentor to develop goals for the next six to 12 months. They were encouraged to use data to inform these goals. The process was rolled out to students in a way that was deliberate, cognisant of the fact that students had not seen the data visualised in that way before and may not immediately have understood what they were looking at.

In the mentoring meetings, students discussed their goals, what they saw in the data they had been presented and the next steps that they planned to take. The mentor teacher had, prior to the meeting, been shown how to read and interpret the information, and had perused each student's data. During the meeting, the mentor teacher shared things they noticed in the data, reflected on the student's goals and facilitated a conversation with the student. The mentor helped guide and refine goals and actions where necessary. By the end of the meeting, students and the mentor teacher would record specific goals that the student would be working towards.

This process was completed three times during Year 12, and students met with the same mentor teacher each time. At first, some mentors – those who did not feel working with data was their strength – sought guidance on how to have the conversations and what they might look like, because they were determined to 'get it right' and do a good job for their students. To support the process, members of the team held lunchtime sessions and modelled conversations, and provided supporting documentation and guidance with tips and tricks for the mentor teachers. The mentors realised very quickly that they could do it and do it well. Some even reflected that, as teachers, we talk with students all day every day that we are at work; adding data to the goal-setting conversation just provided some tangible evidence of how the student had been achieving up until that point.

The process was really successful. Most importantly, it provided a specific, formal and targeted goal-setting conversation for students, informed by data. Students reported that they enjoyed the conversations with their mentors, and that they left with a much better understanding of where they were at with their learning and achievement.

SMART goal conversations in primary school

The previous example pertained to senior school students; however, we know that deliberate conversations about student achievement and progress are not limited to secondary schools, and can happen at all levels, if done in a way that is age appropriate. One of my favourite primary school examples that I have come across to date is from a teacher named Sylvia, who has SMART goal (see Doran 1981) conversations with her Year 3 and 4 students.

Sylvia invited me to come into her classroom and see the work she had been doing with her students on setting goals. She showed me the goal-setting wall, where each student had a laminated card with their name on it, on which they could put two sticky notes showing their goals – one for each half of the year (see figure 9).

Figure 9: Student goals on the wall in a Year 3 and 4 composite classroom

I was immediately impressed by the specificity and detail evident in the students' goals. I asked Sylvia what she had done to get the students to a point were they were able to write goals in this way.

She took me to a student's workbook, where she opened to a page that showed a SMART goal template, which helped students set goals that were specific, measurable, achievable, relevant and time-bound (see figure 10). As they were devising their goal, students articulated on the template how the goal would meet the SMART goal expectations. Once they had done this thinking and had finalised their goal in their books, they discussed their goal with Sylvia. Sylvia supported the process by talking to them about what they had written and how she thought they could refine their goal, and they would make any adjustments that they needed to. Once they had agreed on the process, students could write their goal on the sticky note and post it on the wall.

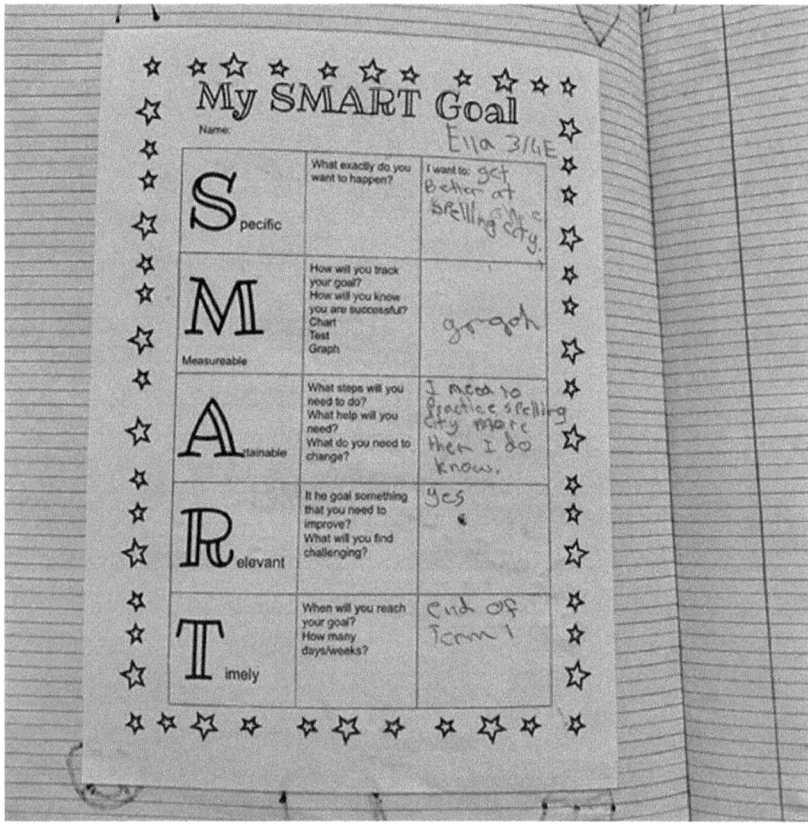

Figure 10: SMART goal template in student book

This process undoubtedly took Sylvia time to set up and establish in her classroom. However, she saw the value in doing so, and in having conversations with students about where they were at and what they were aiming to do next. Sylvia reported that the second time she did this activity with a group of students it was quicker than the first, as students had their previous goals to go back to and had already engaged in the process once before.

The school in which I met Sylvia is now having bigger conversations about how to embed goal setting with students across multiple classrooms and year levels, as there is an understanding that if students become used to the process, they will get better at it (and quicker!) over time. It will then not take as long for each teacher to set it up in their classroom.

Student co-constructed goals with the teacher

Sylvia's example above highlights what can be achieved when students are guided to make decisions and have conversations about their goals and next steps in their learning. A similar example of a lower primary school teacher and their students comes from teacher Nic, who co-constructs student goals with each of her students.

As shown in figure 11, each student was given a piece of paper on which, during a meeting with their teacher, they would detail and document what they were working towards in their learning. These goals were unique to each student, and took on a range of granularity and areas, including mathematics, specific times tables, analogue time, reading with expression, spelling and cursive writing.

Figure 11: Example of teacher and student co-constructed goals in lower primary

The thing that I particularly like about this example is that there are goals that students wrote that are not directly related to traditional 'learning analytics' or literacy and numeracy – including neat writing, listening and being kind. Although I was not present during these meetings, the students' goals reflect what this teacher values – students being good humans and friends, as well as being learners. What an incredibly powerful and important message that is to our students.

Chapter 9

Intersection E: Goal setting and data on walls

Another way that goal setting can occur in class time is through students self-reporting their level of skill or understanding on a data wall in the classroom. When this occurs, a learning goal, descriptors of success criteria or a proficiency scale are featured on the wall. Students self-report by posting an image or their name next to the level of proficiency achieved. I have seen this practice used more often in primary schools rather than secondary schools, but I don't see a reason as to why it would be used more frequently in one setting than the other. Although secondary school teachers often do not have the same classroom for all of their classes, it is still possible to use this approach when all of the timetabled lessons for a class are in the same place.

For students to self-report their comfort with a particular skill or topic, they need a way of representing their position on the continuum. One of the things that you will need to consider is how students will show their position. Here are some ways this might be done:

- Students write their name on a piece of paper on the wall.
- Students write their name on a laminated/wipeable wall, which allows them to move their name as they need to.

- Students have a card with their school photo that they can attach to the wall. Other options for the photo include a photo of the student that you/they have taken in class (this could be a fun photo with props!); a picture students have drawn of themselves (with or without their name); or a shape, animal or icon (again, with or without their name).

Involving students in the process of developing their own card incorporates their interests and individual preferences into the activity. I visited a school that had student cards where students were given masks and capes so they could pose as superheros. Another had animal masks and allowed students to choose their animal and their pose.

It is also worth considering the level of transparency with the data cards. If they have been drawn by the student, you may choose to ask them to put their name on the card, leave their name off, or make writing their name on the card optional. The times that I have done this I have made the name optional; but within a short time, and with a culture of psychological safety in the room about discussing progress and achievement, students added their names within two weeks.

Prep goal-setting wall

I saw a great example of a teacher using goal setting on data walls in her classroom in North Queensland. The teacher had worked with students to set goals – one for literacy and one for numeracy – and she wrote all of their goals on individual cards and put them on the wall. In this class of prep students (four to five-year-olds) all were able to talk about what they were working on next, and the specific next steps that they had discussed with their teacher. As a result, students understood where they were at and what they needed to do to improve, and they were celebrated when they achieved their goals.

As shown in figure 12, there were two types of goals. Literacy goals were on the left, represented by stars; and numeracy goals were on the right, represented by turtles. Some of the literacy goals included:

- *Harleigh*: Sounds: u, v, q, x and letters: h, y, u, q, x
- *Brooklyn*: s, a, t, p, i, n
- *Beau*: Sounds: y, u, x and a sight words set

Some of the numeracy goals included:

- *Andrea*: Count backwards from 20 to 1 and count in 10s
- *Mackenzie*: Identify 20, 15, 9, 18, 19
- *Deejay*: Identify 12, Count 1–20 and count backwards from 10–0

Figure 12: The literacy and numeracy goal data wall in a prep classroom

The thing that I particularly liked about this approach was the positive way that the teacher went about promoting the goals and successes. The language on the board, such as 'we are amazing', 'learn something new' and 'we choose positivity', sends a clear message about viewing learning and goals as something positive and worthwhile.

In their regular meetings with the teacher, students ticked off the elements of the goals that they were able to do (and you can see this on many of the stars and turtles in this image). Further, when the student achieved all the components of the goal, the teacher copied the star or turtle and sent it home with a note to the student's parents/guardians, celebrating the achievement their child had experienced.

Wellbeing tree

In a Year 10 to 12 vocational school that I visited, the Year 12 tutor group had a wellbeing wall in their classroom that students contributed to daily (see figure 13). The school started the day with a circle discussion about how students were feeling, and how they were showing up to school and their learning that day. Students were encouraged to use common words to describe how they were feeling, such as:

- confident
- energetic
- chilled
- happy
- motivated
- anxious
- tired
- stressed
- angry.

Figure 13: The wellbeing tree in a Year 12 tutor group room

When students came into the room at the beginning of the day, prior to the circle conversation, they were encouraged to take a coloured dot and place it on the wall to represent how they were feeling. Through the circle conversation, they would talk about where they placed their dot and how they were travelling, only sharing with the group what they were comfortable with. At the end of the dot exercise and circle discussion, the teacher talked with students about the trends he saw in the wellbeing visualisation on the wall. As you can see in the figure there were students in all parts of the tree when I visited, but there were significant numbers in the 'chilled' and 'happy' categories. However, there were also some students who identified that they were feeling angry or tired. This would lead to a conversation about how we look out for others when they are feeling this way.

The coloured dots de-identified the data in some ways, as students did not have to put their name to a feeling on the wall, and they did not have to share in the circle if they did not want to; however, many did share where they positioned themselves and what was going on for them.

The dots stayed on the wall and accumulated throughout the week, before being removed at the beginning of the following week when the conversation would start afresh. This was partly due to the teacher trying to start with a 'clean slate' each week; but also, in the early days, it was an important part of the conversation about normalising the fact that some weeks will be different, and different students will have different challenges at different times. We just need to be aware of what is going on for ourselves and others.

Shoelace tying in a Year 1 classroom

I experienced my very first data wall when I was in Year 1. Our teacher decided to make learning to tie shoelaces a competition and a goal that we aspired to, and our progress was shared on the wall in our classroom. (I'm sure the teacher chose this goal because she was sick of tying our shoelaces for us!)

Our names were on individual cards on the wall. We all started together, on the left-hand side – these were the students who could not tie their shoelaces. On the right-hand side, there was a bright, colourful, laminated cartoon image of a shoe, with the heading 'I can tie my shoes!'. Given that I was six years old at the time, I do not remember the way the teacher explained it to us, or what she said; however, I do remember the way it motivated me to have my name move onto the laminated shoe – preferably before anyone else!

I couldn't tie my shoes at this point, but having understood the challenge, I decided that I was going to spend my night having my dad teach me how to do it. As many six-year-olds do, I got home and totally forgot; I did what I normally did after school, and the data wall didn't enter my mind. When I arrived at school the next day, the teacher announced that we had our first students who could tie their shoelaces! They came to the front of the room, demonstrated their new skill and their names were moved onto the image of the shoe. They were chuffed... I was not! How could I have forgotten?! How did I let others beat me?! So, I resolved to go home and learn, so I could quickly join them on the honour roll the next day.

The next morning came around, the teacher mentioned shoelaces, and I realised that I had forgotten for a second time! A few more students got up, demonstrated their skill and made it onto the shoe. I was gutted. However, as disappointed as I was, I kept forgetting, and this pattern repeated itself for a couple of days, until more than half the class were on the shoe image. I was getting more frustrated with myself for forgetting, and more motivated to remember.

Eventually I remembered to get my dad to teach me how to tie my shoelaces, and I proudly went into class the next day, chuffed with my new skill, and saw my name move onto the shoe.

For me as a learner this was an incredibly motivating activity, and it made my learning (or lack of it) visible. I am aware that I am a competitive person, and this type of comparison was particularly helpful for me; but it did pique my interest in learning the skill, particularly when I could see some of my peers had developed the skill before me.

I had a similar experience with my pen license in Year 6... But you probably don't need to hear that story – it goes much the same!

Chapter 10

Intersection F: Behaviour or learner dispositions and data walls

The next intersection considers behaviour or learner dispositions, and having the information on data walls. Like intersection A (and K, which we'll cover soon), this intersection is not as common as some of the others in the book; but it does occur, and it can be beneficial if we are willing to give it a go.

Attendance data wall

In my first book, *Using and Analysing Data in Australian Schools,* I provided an example of a data wall that had been used with students in a flexible learning context that showed young people's attendance. For this data wall, student attendance was grouped into specific categories relating to the attendance percentage, and the data wall was constructed on a board that was moveable. The data wall was taken to assembly and used in conversation with students at the beginning of every week.

The categories on the data wall reflected the different zones of attendance: very high attendance was in dark green at the top of the board; high attendance was light green; yellow sat in the middle of the board; and the attendance percentages below this were orange and red. Every Friday, a school officer would take each of the data cards for the students, erase the previous attendance percentage, write the new values on and reposition students on the data wall. On Mondays, school leaders would take the board to assembly and recognise and celebrate the students who had attended at a high level (that is, students who were in the light or dark green categories).

The attendance percentages were reset at the beginning of each term, because if a student missed a lot of school early on in the year their percentage would be affected for the entire year, even if they started to come to school regularly. I have seen other teachers and schools reset the attendance percentage more frequently, such as weekly or at the end of each five-week block.

The conversation around this data wall was had in a safe space, and it was framed as 'this is actually about you and we want to support you', and 'we want you at school because we want you to be successful'. This approach facilitated a conversation that was open and transparent. Teachers became more confident in talking to young people about their attendance, and students had a much better understanding of what their attendance was and why it mattered. In addition, the school leader did a good job of articulating the impact of missing one day per week and what it would mean if a young person was to do that over their entire schooling career.

In *Using and Analysing Data in Australian Schools* I discussed that this approach of using a data wall at an assembly may not be for everyone, and that is okay. There may be instances where you choose to modify this approach; for example, by only identifying students in the yellow category and above, or removing particular students from the data wall who have complex situations that are contributing to their low attendance but are beyond their control. You could also use this strategy at a year-level assembly or in class, particularly in schools where cohorts are too large to have one data wall for the whole school.

The culture and climate of care you create, and the way in which you articulate that you want to bring students along on the journey with you, will ultimately determine whether or not this strategy is successful. If you have good relationships with your students and your teachers, this could be a highly effective and useful strategy for you to use.

Classroom attendance tracking

Attendance is a major challenge for many educators. The following is an example of a context I visited where they were trying to get students to school and wanted to have regular conversations with students about their attendance.

The teacher created a data wall that showed every student in the class (down the left) and each week of the term (across the top). At the end of each week, the teacher would calculate the attendance percentage for each student and would colour each cell in the table with a different-coloured whiteboard marker (see figure 14). The categories were:

- red for attendance under 30 per cent
- orange for 31–40 per cent
- pink for 41–50 per cent
- blue for 51–80 per cent
- green for above 80 per cent.

Attendance was a major challenge for this cohort, and a number of students attended under 50 per cent of the time. This approach enabled educators to have a targeted and specific conversation with their students at the beginning of the week about their attendance in the previous week, and throughout the term.

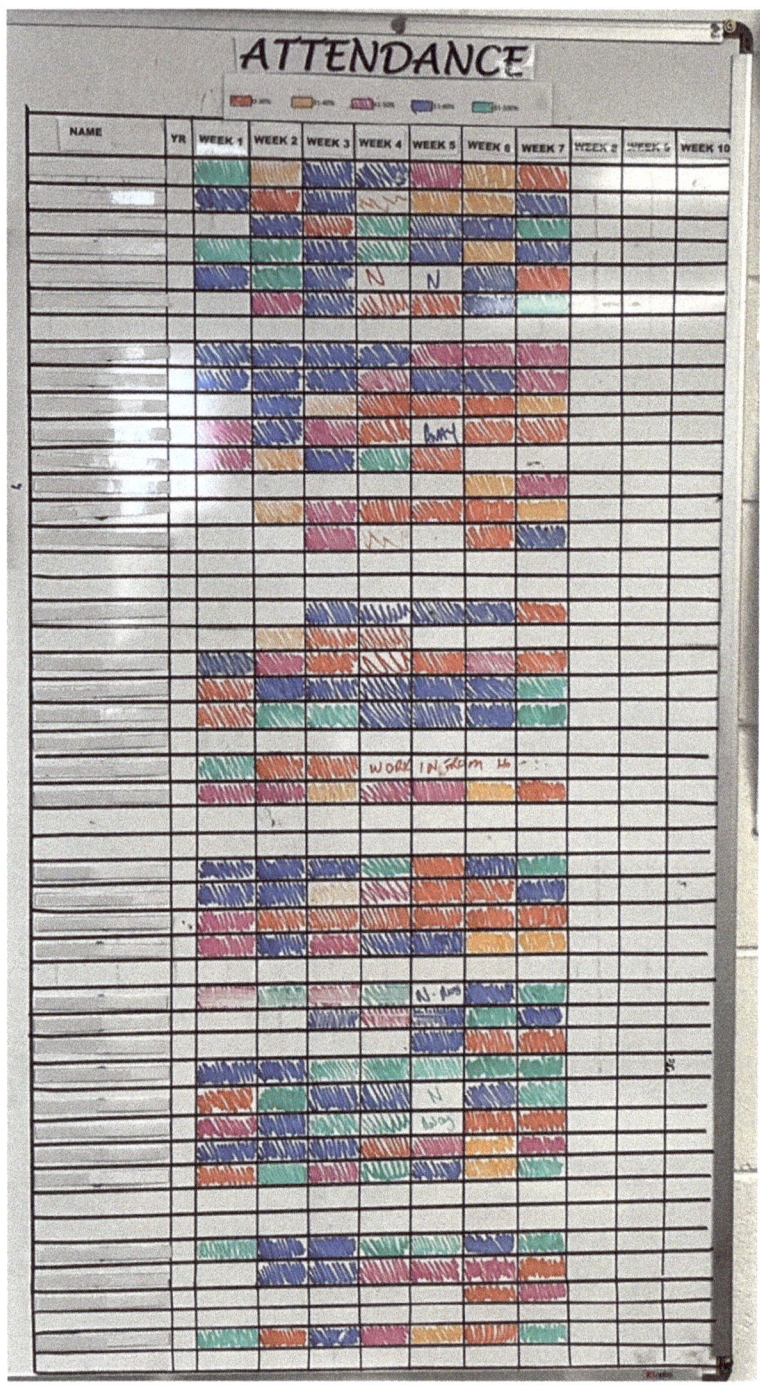

Figure 14: Data wall showing weekly colour-coded attendance for each young person

The educators also implemented a rewards system, shown in figure 15. If students had 'green' attendance in the previous week, or had improved their level of attendance from any level, educators could celebrate and reward those students. If their attendance was lower than the previous week, it provided an opportunity for educators to have a conversation about was going on for the student and see if they could support the student in any way.

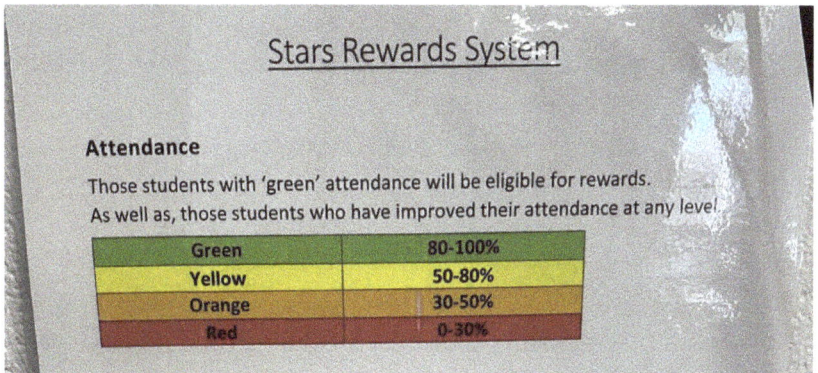

Figure 15: Associated rewards levels for attendance

Berry Street dashboard – student wellbeing and readiness to learn

Berry Street School is a flexible learning context in Victoria. A small but mighty part of the Berry Street Education Model is a daily check-in where students talk about how they are feeling and how ready they are to learn. At the beginning of each day, teachers ask these two questions of students, and students give a score on a 1–5 scale for each question. In the past, this data was shown on walls in the room or shared in conversations with staff. Teachers felt this was a really useful process, and it enabled them to understand where each young person was at, each day; however, the school reflected that this data was often 'lost', and trends for individual young people, classes and campuses were not obvious or able to be retained. Much of the data on the walls was reset each day, and inevitably, teachers could only remember a limited amount of the information that students were providing.

Consequently, the Principal and data team sought to create a way to electronically collect this information and share it daily with key staff in a dashboard. They did this by creating an online form, using the same two questions and the five-point scale. Each day, to either accompany the conversation or, in some cases, replace it, students logged into their iPads, entered the form and selected the values that showed how they were that day. Because students were logged into their Microsoft accounts, the result was attached to them as a unique user.

The conversation still occurred at the classroom level in some form or another, but the electronic entry of the data formalised the collection and meant that visualisations could be developed. As shown in figure 16, there were visual cues on the wall about the different levels, including some key words and emotions for each of the five 'feelings'. Although this was a regular practice and students were used to the process, teachers had conversations with young people when they needed to about how to respond.

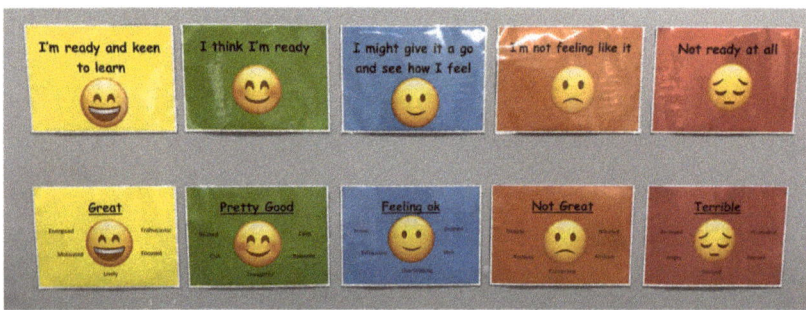

Figure 16: Readiness to learn scale and general feeling scale in one classroom at Berry Street School

Through an application processing interface (API), the data that the young people entered on the online form was automatically fed into two dashboards (see figure 17) that were created for the school staff, using Power BI (which is a Microsoft product). The dashboards updated at a few key points each day, which allowed staff to access recent entries from students, regardless of the time they arrived at school and completed the survey. Staff could see results for individual students each day, but they could also see student trends over time – for example, if a student began reporting differently to how they had been previously, or how consistent their results were over time.

The wellbeing team was the main group of staff that had access to this dashboard, and they checked student results daily. They would generally follow up with students (and their teachers) who entered a '1' or a '2' for how they were feeling, or how ready they were to learn (although this was not a hard-and-fast rule).

Troy, one of the teachers at Berry Street, said that it was a useful tool to use – it meant young people had a more private way of letting staff know how they were feeling; they began to see that follow-up would occur; and it helped them feel seen. He said that it was a good conversation starter with students who were reporting positive results in the dashboards but did not seem to be going all that well in class. It also provided specific information that staff could use with parents and caregivers, which allowed them to have a targeted conversation about how each young person was travelling.

Figure 17: Example dashboard with the wellbeing survey data

Chapter 11

Intersection G: Behaviour or learner dispositions and success criteria

When I first started working with the model of purpose and mode for engaging students in their data story, and thinking about the different intersections, intersection G and H were difficult to populate. However, the more I did this work with teachers in different schools, the more I was exposed to different ideas around using data with students in these ways. I'm grateful that the teachers I worked with expanded my understanding of what was possible and how data could be used in these spaces.

Learner dispositions tracking in a vocational subject

Greg, the teacher who shared this example of tracking with me, initially told me that he did not use data in his work. When I first met him, in a training session where I asked participants about their beliefs on data, he told me that he did not believe in data because he taught certificate courses in a workshop, and the use of data was not applicable to him. He believed that standardised assessments and previous results were not relevant – they often did not tell him whether a student would succeed, because many of the assessments did not measure the skills that were valued in his field.

Fast forward a few hours into the activity I was running, and Greg said to me, 'Well, Selena, I do have a few spreadsheets of things that I track. Would you like to take a look?'. Needless to say, Greg *did*, in fact, collect and use a lot of data, and this example (and another in intersection L) came from him.

In senior vocational courses, students need to demonstrate a range of learner dispositions throughout the course. They are required to demonstrate knowledge of safety, attitudes and skills to stay safe in the workplace, and ensure not only that they complete the competencies satisfactorily, but that they will be safe and efficient workers on a job site. Students also need to demonstrate consistency in their approach – not demonstrate a skill once, but demonstrate it on a regular basis. Greg decided that the easiest way to track when students did not show up as they should was to create a spreadsheet that recorded the dates that lapses, or gaps in training, had been observed.

As figure 18 shows, some of the learner dispositions Greg tracked were arriving on time, having all required equipment at hand, working consistently and doing work safely at all times. Every student had this table on a separate tab in the spreadsheet, and Greg would enter, when he needed to, dates that the gap in training was observed. As noted in the 'instructions' section, students were told when an entry was made so they were aware of the gap, and students could access a read-only version of this document at all times. Greg said that it helped him stay on top of where students were at; but more importantly, it supported evidence-informed conversations with students and parents/guardians about how students were showing up to lessons, what challenges or gaps there were and what was required to achieve competence.

Behaviour or learner dispositions and success criteria

		MARIST COLLEGE EMERALD			
		MEM20413 - Certificate II in Engineering Pathways			
		OBSERVATION Checklist - GAP BOOK			
		Refer to the Marist College MEM20413 Planning Overview for referencing of Units, Elements and Performance Criteria			
Student:		Assessor:		Period of Observation:	

Assessment Conditions: These observations and demonstrations involve the knowledge, attitude and skills required to undertake routine tasks; to work safely in a manufacturing environment; to apply principles of OH&S in the workshop and to apply quality procedures consistently throughout the course of each project and in general conduct while in the workplace.

Instructions: The assessor will identify any areas where the student has observed gaps in the practical skills, safe working habits and quality procedures indicated and provide feedback to the student immediately via verbal communication. A date will indicate where a gap has been identified. No date indicates a student is on track to achieving competence. Students are to have access to this form and can review any comments and observations

Line	Observed or Demonstrated Activities	Dates Gaps in Training Observed — Assessment Items — 2 4 5 8 9 10 11 14 15 16 18 19 20
1	Arrive on time	
2	Have all required equipment at hand	
3	Be well presented, neat and tidy	
4	Appropriate language used	
5	Working consistently	
6	Work is carried out safely at all times	

Figure 18: Example of learner dispositions tracking

Alice Springs engagement levels

Joanne Alford is the Principal of Centralian Secondary College, Alice Springs, and the former Principal of Berry Street School, which we discussed in the previous chapter. For the students that Joanne has worked with in the last few years of her career, it is probably fair to say that learning analytics have not been the most important data set. In complex scenarios and contexts, Jo has focused instead on learner dispositions – partly so she could have targeted conversations with students and parents/guardians about the things that matter, but also so young people could build good habits that would support their academic success.

Jo and her staff wanted to more formally document the progress and levels that students were at in their readiness to learn. They constructed a matrix of key indicators and levels of success (shown in figure 19). Some of the factors included engagement, respectful relationships and emotion regulation.

Readiness to Learn Scope and Sequence

The purpose of the scope and sequence is to provide explicit knowledge of the behaviour barriers, learning readiness and skills to be taught so that students who have been disengaged from education for a considerable time can be taught the skills necessary and set goals to help them manage their learning journey (education)

	No access	Significantly disengaged	Partly engaged	Moderately engaged	Engaged	Very engaged	Outreach/when a child disengages
Body							
Self-Regulation	Not yet able to self regulate, intense unpredictable reactions, and does not have strategies for impulse control.	Is not yet able to regulate his/her emotions and does not have strategies to do so. Experiences ongoing chaos and crisis.	Is not yet able to effectively regulate his/her emotions. Listens to strategies to regulate emotions.	Has identified strategies to regulate emotions however he/she finds it difficult to consistently do so.	Is able to effectively utilise strategies to regulate his/her emotions.	Uses a range of strategies to regulate emotions with success even during stressful situations.	Possible life event has triggered disengagement, possible drug abuse or decline of mental health. Over time, through outreach using positive relationships will re-engage. Novelty re engagement activities required. May be able to discuss level and state of emotions.
De-escalation Strategies	High risk factors impacting students life.	Not yet completed their focus plan.	Not yet able to utilise their focus plan.	Completed the focus plan and utilises the plan to some extent.	Completed the focus plan and modifies it effectively.	Completed the focus plan, utilises and modifies it regularly.	Will understand the language used for de-escalation, may be able to articulate their frustration and emotional state.
Relationships							
Peer Relationships	Relationships within school not yet developed.	Is withdrawn from others and not yet able to establish positive relationships with peers.	Relationships are impacted by over sensitive responses, chaos and crisis. Has some negative relationships that require repairing and generally avoids most peers.	Relates well to a small group of peers at school with similar life views. Beginning to develop these relationships with some adults too.	Usually relates well to all students.	Relates positively with a wide range of students at school.	Initially 1 to 1 followed by restorative practice, may respond to key peer positive relationships to re-engage.
Cooperation	Substance abuse, possible mental health concerns, major dysfunction.	Is disruptive and uncooperative or very passive.	At times disruptive and uncooperative or passive.	Generally cooperates with others, but is occasionally disruptive.	Generally cooperates with others.	Very cooperative with others and supportive of them.	Will slowly respond to key staff relationship to encourage re-engagement. May be reliant on well-known staff and find transition challenging.

Behaviour or learner dispositions and success criteria

Figure 19: The learner disposition matrix

There were five levels in each of the indicators, and students were tracked along the continuum. Jo shared with me that when a young person went from not going to school at all, to going to school but sitting in the corridor, to entering a classroom, then eventually to engaging in learning, huge growth had occurred. The systems and processes that the school had in place prior to this matrix did not make this progress visible to young people, parents/guardians or teachers.

Staff at her previous and current school use the results of this matrix and the levels of successful engagement in conversation with students and with parents/guardians. It means they have more tangible goals and a vision for success, and progress up the levels is an opportunity for recognition and celebration.

Clontarf program – success criteria on the classroom wall

The Clontarf Foundation supports young Indigenous men to finish school and gain employment (see clontarf.org.au). When I visited the Clontarf space in Alice Springs, one of the things that stood out to me was a version of success criteria on the classroom wall. Unlike other classrooms or contexts, this data wall showed the indicators of success that all students were working towards, and it tracked student completion across the different elements. Unlike curriculum expectations, all the elements demonstrated the competencies that the program was working towards to ensure students were ready and prepared to enter the workforce.

As shown in figure 20, some of the attributes of success that were identified were a completed résumé, bank account, Medicare card, driver's licence and so on. As students completed each element, it was ticked off and recorded on the classroom wall. This method of tracking provided a clear statement of what was valued in the program and what students were working towards, as well as a clear visual representation of where students were at. Looking at the table allowed teachers to ascertain which elements individual students had completed, as well being able to identify consistent gaps across the group.

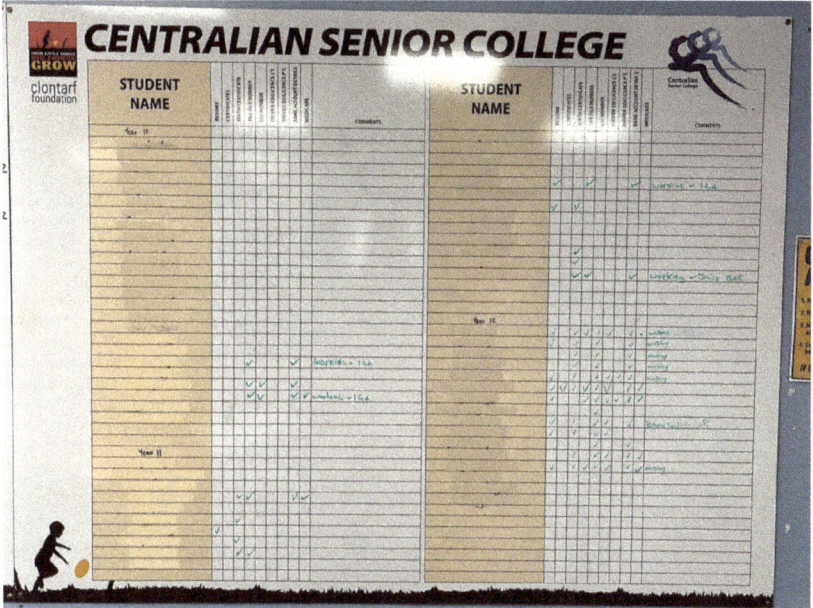

Figure 20: Clontarf tracking table

Chapter 12

Intersection H: Behaviour or learner dispositions and student-generated assessment

Like this previous intersection, this is not used as frequently as some of the other intersections in part 3. Having students generate assessment for behaviour or learner dispositions is not common; however, it does occur and it can be a powerful way of having students buy into how they will be assessed in a completely different domain to the more traditional learning analytics. As with assessment tasks, there are formative and summative versions and options for this approach. This chapter offers examples of both formative and summative use of this data.

CHeck In and CHeck Out (CHICHO) cards

In many schools that I have worked in, students with behaviour challenges were placed on behaviour cards and were often managed by middle or senior leaders in the school. In the most recent school that I worked in, they were called CHICHO cards, as these students had to 'CHeck In and CHeck Out' each day.

These behaviour cards were a good example of behaviour or learner disposition factors and student-generated assessment, used in a way that was formative. Although the approach had an element of guiding or support from the teacher who was managing the student, often students would design the way they would be assessed or graded by teachers in each lesson.

In the case of the CHICHO cards, students had three things that would be 'marked' by each of their teachers, on a four-point scale. Students had to choose goals that related to behaviours or learner dispositions that they had previously struggled with. Common goals on the cards included things such as:

- arriving to class on time
- bringing all required equipment
- speaking respectfully to teachers
- staying in the classroom for the whole lesson
- completing homework
- having a charged laptop.

Each lesson, teachers gave a score from 0–3 for each of the goals:

- 0: not demonstrated at all
- 1: inconsistent
- 2: good
- 3: great.

From each teacher, students could get a maximum score of nine points, and across the six period day, 54 points. Each afternoon, students would check in with their case manager and they would talk through the scores: what had gone well, and what needed to be improved as they moved forward. Parents/guardians signed the cards each night to confirm that they had seen them, and the goals were modified at the beginning of each week if needed.

This was a powerful process because students had co-constructed the goals with staff, meaning these expectations were not something being put on the students. They had identified the areas they wanted to work on. This meant that students were more connected to the process, they took it more seriously, and it was much more useful to them than being assigned generic expectations or goals.

Reporting on effort, behaviour and homework

On many school report cards, teachers give students a 'grade' for factors other than traditional learning analytics. Some common examples include:

- effort
- behaviour
- homework completion
- engagement
- participation.

Schools often ask teachers to score students on a scale, and these scales vary across sites. Some of the examples I've seen are:

- a grade of A–E
- a score of 1–5 (5 being the highest)
- a descriptive scale (for example: consistently, sometimes, rarely, never).

One of the most common concerns I hear from teachers is about the validity and reliability of the scores that teachers have given students. This is often amplified by the fact that often, these different levels do not have a specific descriptor, or descriptors exist but are not regularly referred to or shared with new staff. This means that assessing students can be incredibly subjective – especially considering different learner attributes, if not detailed, can mean different things to different teachers).

An alternate to having levels that teachers struggle to agree on is to involve students in the discussion about what the different levels look like. There needs to be consistency across departments or year levels, but students can, and are often good at being able to, co-construct what a learner at each level looks like.

Although this might not be done as frequently as other practices mentioned throughout this book, I have seen it happen in schools for summative reporting, where students have the capacity to engage in the conversation. In my Year 11 Mathematics class, I used to ask students what level of homework completion would be reflective of 'always', 'usually', 'sometimes' or 'rarely' (I would track this in a spreadsheet). As a class, we agreed to at least 90 per cent completion for always, 70 per cent for usually and 50 per cent for sometimes, with less than 50 per cent meaning rarely. We had this conversation at the beginning of the year, and students often referred to the cut-off percentages as they knew I was tracking them. The report card grade was not the be-all and end-all, but the structure and the conversation meant that students felt they had control over the result they would receive. If they wanted to complete or catch up on homework later in the term to get themselves into the next grade boundary, I would always let them do so. I felt it was a win-win – they completed the work they had missed and had valuable opportunities to build skill and understanding in the subject, and they were rewarded with a better result on their report card.

I presented a session on data-informed learners prior to writing this book, and a teacher came to me at the end of the session, after I had said this intersection is not used very often. She shared with me that she co-constructed success criteria with students in each of her classes regarding expectations of their behaviour and learning when she was away. She led a conversation with each of her classes about what learning looks like, and how students should engage in learning when she was absent and there was a cover teacher. Each class had its own set of descriptors outlining what the supply teacher should expect from the students. She left a note for the supply teacher explaining what students had agreed to and asking for feedback specifically on the 'assessment' that students had committed to. It enabled her to have a conversation with students when she returned that was specific to what students had created themselves, and committed to. The teacher reported that she had also had supply teachers share with her that students had begun moderating other students' behaviour during class – reminding them of what they had agreed to when their usual teacher was away. I thought that was a pretty great example of how having conversations with students about what success looks like can engage them in the process.

Chapter 13

Intersection I: Behaviour or learner dispositions and deliberate conversations

Conversations about behaviour and learner dispositions make up a significant portion of the conversations we have with students. Like in the previous sections regarding conversations, the focus here is on the deliberate and more formal nature of these conversations, rather than informal chats in the classroom or playground. There are, no doubt, endless ways that this can and is done in our schools; however, the following examples provide some ideas that might be a little less common than others.

Checkpoint data for students from Years 6 to 12

While I was researching for this book, Lauren (who is a Deputy Principal in an R–12 school) reached out to me to share her school's practice of having regular and deliberate conversations with students about their progress as learners. One of the first things she mentioned in our chat was the connection between the data analytics processes and learning culture, so I knew this was going to be good.

Once per term, students in Years 6 to 10 complete a survey on learner dispositions, where they self-analyse and reflect on their proficiency in collaboration, creative thinking, critical thinking, personal and social capability, ethical understanding and intercultural understanding. Students are provided with prompts to help them answer the questions, and teachers support students through the process. These reports are intended to provide a holistic view of each student, focusing on academic progress and skills and capabilities. Results are represented in a spider/radar chart (see figure 21) as part of a PDF summary that is provided to the student.

After they answer the questions, students have follow-up conversations with their home group teacher about their report. They identify areas that they are proud of, key learnings, their biggest challenges and what they are working on next. These PDF reports are available on the school's learning management system after the meeting, meaning that parents can see the chart and reflection, and have conversations with their child at home.

Through self analysis, students have evaluated their progress and development in a range of capabilities and skills, by completing a series of questions this week.

This process aims to encourage students to consider areas they can improve in to offer depth and richness to their learning and educational experiences.

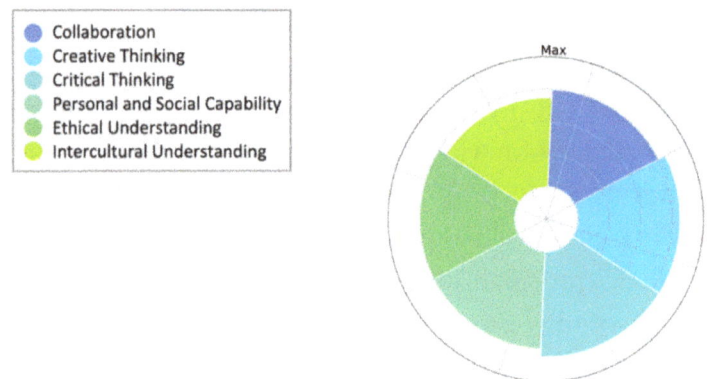

Figure 21: Visualisation from the Year 6 to 10 student report showing learner dispositions

In Year 11 and 12, the focus shifts more to academic performance, and a five-weekly 'checkpoint' activity. While students self-reflect on their results, this model differs to the previous one as the data is entered by classroom teachers. For each subject area, students receive a score out of 40 from their teachers, which is a combination of teacher-generated scores for effort, attendance, formative tasks and summative tasks. As shown in figure 22, the visualisation shows students their score out of 40, and compares their current result to their result from five weeks prior. Showing the data in this way allows for comparison to their own previous performance, as well as across subject areas.

This checkpoint is an opportunity to reflect on your progress in each subject area. Please see below your results out of 40 for each subject.

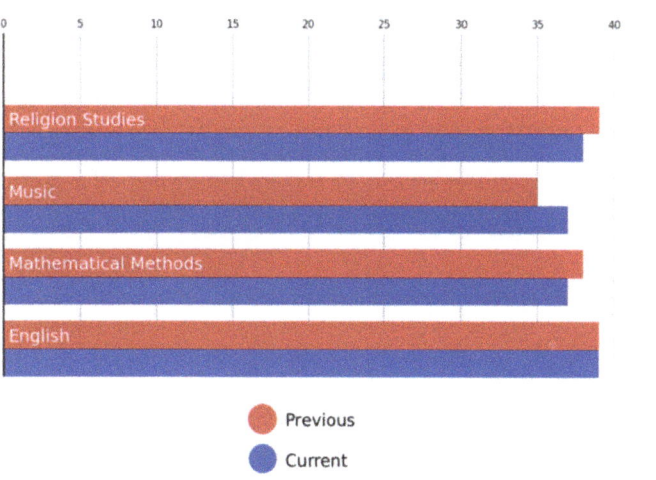

Figure 22: Visualisation from the Year 11 and 12 report showing overall scores for each subject, compared with the previous result

Lauren discussed with me the impact of these processes on the learning environment in the school. She described the high level of student and teacher engagement in the process, the value parents placed on the information they received in the reports, as well as the students' willingness to give feedback to staff about how the process could be enhanced in the future. There are some exciting new changes on the horizon within the school's data analytics model, born out of the students' ideas and contributions.

The process at this school highlights the interconnectedness of learning and wellbeing, with the checkpoints not only a chance to reflect on academic progress, but also pinpointing students in need of additional pastoral support. For staff, the checkpoint became a platform to hold powerful data-informed conversations about how educators support individual students every five weeks. In addition, the impact on the final Year 12 results was hard to argue with – the students attained more 90-plus tertiary entrance rank scores (as well as the highest mean and median tertiary entrance scores) the college had seen in a number of years. The cohort also attained zero D and E grades, with the checkpoint program highlighting early in the year strategic interventions needed for students to improve in subjects they may have been struggling with. Lauren believes that this process supported students through ownership of their learning, and it was motivating and affirming, which led to growth and, consequently, better academic outcomes.

Engagement monitoring and tracking

A trend that I have seen emerging in schools' use of data over the last few years is the increasing desire to track and report on learner dispositions or other elements that are not directly 'learning analytics'. There is increasing recognition and acknowledgement that academic results alone do not define young people; and if we are going to provide them with data and feedback about what really matters, we need to be thinking about the ways in which we do so.

Some schools have worked with the notion of tracking engagement: whether or not students are participating and truly engaging in their lessons. A tool that I have seen used a number of times to support this process is the '5 levels of student engagement' model (shown in table 5) that appears on the TeachThought website (Heick 2022). We discussed this model in chapter 2.

The levels of student engagement model seems to resonate with many teachers, as it outlines the important distinction between compliance and authentic engagement. Further, it provides a descriptor of what student behaviour looks like at each level and, given that it is on a five-point scale, it provides a way for teachers to position students on this continuum and 'assess' them.

Table 5: '5 levels of student engagement' model (from Heick 2022, based on work by Schlechty 2002)

Level	Characterised by
Engagement	Persistence, sustained inquiry, self-direction, playfulness with content and unprompted transfer of understanding.
Strategic compliance	Clear effort; some creativity; focus on directions and task completion to meet extrinsic standards for motivation.
Ritual compliance	Minimal effort made only to mitigate 'consequences' or other negative 'punishers'; no creativity, genius, curiosity or transfer.
Retreatism	Little to no effort, productivity or progress; no demonstrated inquiry, affection or interest in the content, collaborations or task.
Rebellion	Zero demonstration of learning; outright disruption and defiance.

I have seen this model (and others like it) used a few different ways in schools:

- Some schools have adopted the model as is, and had teachers report on student engagement; however, students were not involved in the process, other than to see an overall score on their report card at the end of the semester.
- Some schools have adapted the language in the descriptors to make it more contextually relevant and useful for them. By doing so, they felt the language resonated with teachers and they were more likely to engage with the process and understand the nuance between the levels.
- Some schools have taken the approach of giving students scores on the scale a couple of times per term. This has meant that students have 'average' results for specific subject areas, and across all of their subjects. This data can be used in mentoring conversations throughout the year.
- Some schools have fed the information into visualisation dashboards, so teachers and students can see student engagement levels alongside more traditional learning analytics measures such as academic grades, attendance and standardised assessment. The information could also be used in mentoring conversations alongside the learning analytics data.
- Some schools have involved students in the process, asking them to self-assess against the levels, as well as teaching staff giving them scores.

It seems that this work really lands when students self-assess on the rubric and teachers give a rating for each student; *and* a facilitated conversation follows between the teacher and students about their perceptions. Teachers who have done this have told me that it has been a good opportunity to have a conversation with their class about what engagement actually is, and to open up dialogue about the difference between engagement and compliance.

At an individual level, this method provides an opportunity to discuss similarities and differences between the score that the student gave themselves compared with how the teacher assessed them, and to unpack reasons as to why any differences exist. These conversations, whether they be individual or with a class group, also provide an opportunity for students to set goals, understand more about the characteristics of an engaged learner and be reflective about their reality.

Wellbeing surveys at Brigidine College Indooroopilly

Student wellbeing surveys have become much more common in schools post-pandemic. Many schools used to have students complete annual bullying and/or general school surveys, but increasingly, schools are having students regularly self-report on their wellbeing. There are wellbeing survey applications on the market that schools can buy. All of these visualise the data for teachers, and some allow integration into school visualisation tools. Alternatively, some schools create their own surveys using products they already have access to (such as Microsoft or Google forms) and connect to visualisation tools that demonstrate trends (such as Power BI, Tableau or Google Sites) alongside other learning analytics and student details.

Brigidine College Indooroopilly, Queensland set out to develop its own student wellbeing survey, which it runs with students twice per term. After an initial trial of the process and the first version of questions, the wellbeing team learned what worked and did not work in their context, and set out to run a more effective and efficient second version.

Prior to implementation of the second iteration, under the guidance of the Dean of Student Formation, the house leaders spent a lot of time deciding what they would ask, how they would collect the information, what they would do with it and how it would be used. The team devoted plenty of energy to drafting, rewriting and consulting on questions to ensure they would achieve what they were setting out to do.

Prior to the release of the survey questions to students, the team organised the processes for rollout and the workflow for analysing and prioritising the data and students, and identified specific ways they would intervene when they saw data that was concerning. It was vital that they had the process right before the release to students, as they did not want a student to report or disclose something that was concerning without staff knowing about it and acting quickly.

A general outline of the process that they used was as follows:

1. Process/outline for the wellbeing survey collection shared with teaching staff at the beginning of the week (Monday briefing/staff meeting).
2. All students complete wellbeing survey in the same homeroom lesson in the week prior to the scheduled teaching staff's House Meeting (on Tuesday or Wednesday).
3. School Officer follows up and completes catch-ups on the following days. Homeroom teachers are encouraged to support the catch-ups to develop relationships with students.
4. School Officer completes agreed analysis and sends spreadsheet with priority students highlighted to pastoral leaders by 3 pm Friday.
5. House leaders analyse summary house data sent from School Officer by end of Monday and identify students requiring follow-up by homeroom teachers.

6. House leaders present to homeroom teachers the list of students requiring a follow-up conversation in pastoral meeting (Monday afternoon).
7. Homeroom teachers follow up on identified students by Wednesday afternoon of the same week. They place an entry for each conversation in the student's online record and make contact with the pastoral leader, student's teachers or parents/guardians if required.
8. School Officer develops a school-wide infographic and shares relevant summary data with teachers (checked by Dean of Student Formation).
9. Dean of Student Formation shares the infographic with Formation teachers.
10. Formation teachers share the school-wide infographic and relevant data with students in formation lessons, facilitating a conversation about the data.
11. Dean of Student Formation shares the school-wide infographic and relevant data with parents/guardians via blog posts and Facebook account.

The school decided to structure all survey questions in the same way to minimise confusion. They decided the best way to do this was to have students report, on a five-point scale, to what extent they agreed with a list of statements. The statements that students responded to were as follows:

- I have generally felt good/positive over the last week.
- I have generally felt productive with my learning over the last week.
- I have generally slept well over the last week.
- I am generally happy with how much I have moved my body in the last week.

- I am generally happy in my interactions with peers over the last week.
- I usually feel I belong, am accepted, and acknowledged by my peers at school.
- I usually feel supported, accepted, and acknowledged by staff at school.
- I usually feel secure and supported by my year level.
- I generally feel in control of the time I spend on social media.
- I have the skill to navigate safe interactions online.

These questions were initially grouped into two categories to calculate an overall score for each subsection. One category was actionable by the homeroom teacher with the student directly; the other could be used to inform school-based programs and interventions. As the analysis and use of the data progressed, a third category was added – one which, as the house leaders suggested, was a better indication of whether a student was happy and felt connected at school.

Figure 23 provides a sample visualisation showing the students' average scores from their wellbeing surveys and the most recent scores, alongside learning analytics and attendance.

Although no process is perfect, the school has had some success with the program so far. Teachers have had some good conversations with students, and they are seeing trends over time and with specific cohorts. Although this process will not pick up everything, it is hoped that it is an opportunity for students to reach out if they need to, and that it could possibly help pastoral leaders gain access to a little bit more information than they would have had otherwise.

Behaviour or learner dispositions and deliberate conversations

Student Details			Subject Result		Historic Subject Results			Absences - Yearly Enrolment, 2022		Wellbeing Survey Semester 2 (Semester 2, 2022) : ClosedNotesOnly	
Code	Given Name	Family Name	Semester 1 2022	Trend	Awards 2022	Semester 2 2021	Trend	Absent (All Day)	Late	Wellbeing Survey(Overall)	Wellbeing Survey (04-Oct-2022)
			B-	↗	C+	B	↘	4	1	39	38
			C	↗	C-	B-	↘	18	1	36.5	38
			A-	↗	B+	C+	→	10	5	43	43
			B+	↗	B	B	↘	14	7	30	30
			B	↗	B-	B+	↘	16	3	41	41
			B	↗	B-	A-	↗	13	3	23.5	20
			A	↗	A-	B	↘	9	2	42.5	45
			C+	↗	C	C+	↘	5	10	26	
			B-	↗	C+	C+	↘	14	6	30.5	26
			C	→	C	C+	↘	15	4	33.33	30

Figure 23: Wellbeing survey data triangulated with learning analytics data

Chapter 14

Intersection J: Behaviour or learner dispositions and data on walls

Displaying learner dispositions or behaviour data on classroom walls is not as common as visualising quality of student work data on classroom walls; however, it can be just as powerful. When I first started teaching – in an effort to manage the behaviour of students in my class – I used to do things like count the number of minutes that we would be staying in at lunchtime on the whiteboard, tallying them in the top right corner. In hindsight, I know this probably wasn't all that effective, but it was all I had in my toolkit at the time!

When I realised (and was told by students) that this wasn't a fair system, because the students who were behaving shouldn't have to stay in, I started writing the names of students on the board who would be allowed to leave on time. This approach was perhaps slightly more effective than the tally marks, but it still wasn't great! The examples in this section are far better.

Emojis and behaviour levels on classroom walls

At the beginning of 2020 I presented in a primary school classroom where the teacher had a series of levelled emojis on the wall to show students the different levels of behaviour. There were five levels, with the picture of the emoji on a coloured background:

- The very happy face was on a dark green background.
- The happy face was light green.
- The straight face was yellow.
- The sad face was orange.
- The sad, crying face was red.

Each student had a card with their name on it, and at the beginning of each day, the teacher placed all of their names in the dark green, 'very happy' section. If a student was misbehaving or off-task, the teacher would not say anything publicly, but she would go and move their name to the level below. Immediately, she would go to the student and mention that she had moved their card, and would have a conversation about what they needed to do to improve. Students could visually see on the wall where they sat and where other students were positioned and, ultimately, who was getting closer to a consequence.

There were clear consequences attached to each level. If a student got to the yellow level, it meant that they stayed in briefly at the next break to discuss their behaviour with the teacher. Students in the orange section missed half their next break, and if a student got to the red section, they were immediately removed from the classroom and sent to a buddy room. After the consequence and at the beginning of the next session, the teacher would move them straight back to the dark green section – meaning they had a chance to start again, later in the day.

Although this system may not be for everyone, the thing that I really liked was that the teacher was also happy to move students up the continuum if their behaviour improved, meaning that they moved away from the consequence that they were previously heading towards. When I asked the teacher about how students responded to the movement, she said that if they were dropped down, they would often work hard to get back on track to move back up the continuum.

Behaviour levels in the classroom: Ls, red Ps and green Ps

In a secondary school, I saw a similar strategy to the emojis in the previous example, but with a context that more suited the learners' age group. The theme was learning to drive a car, with L plates for learners, red Ps for P1 provisional drivers and green Ps for P2 provisional drivers (this followed the driver's licence progression system in that state).

The teacher posted a laminated page on the classroom wall, one for each of the coloured categories, showing the plate image on the appropriate page. He created a laminated card for each student that had their name on the front, and students were placed in one of the three categories. When I saw the wall, there was a roughly even distribution of students across the three categories.

I asked the teacher how it was used, and he reported that (unlike the previous emojis example in the primary school) student position on the wall did not tend to change daily, but rather indicated the on-balance or usual level of behaviour of each student. If a student began to show repeatedly positive behaviour and engagement, they would move up from the yellow category (Ls) to the red category (P1) and then to green (P2), but it might take a few days or weeks. Likewise, if their behaviour began to deteriorate over time, the student's position would move down from the green level to the red level, to the yellow. If there was any movement in the cards, the teacher would talk to the student at the time to explain why it was moving.

In this classroom there were different levels of trust and independence attached to each level. If students finished the term in the green Ps, they were able to access positive behaviour rewards and trips. If they were in the Ls stage they had to negotiate where they sat in the classroom with the teacher, but other levels did not have to – they had more flexibility and choice. Students in the red Ps and green Ps were often asked (and trusted) to do class jobs and take on additional responsibility, but L students' behaviour was not always conducive to visiting other classrooms or doing jobs around the school.

The teacher reported that students were very aware of the 'privileges' that came with different levels of behaviour, and it was clear that negative behaviours related to stronger intervention and more rigidity from the teacher. Students understood and could explain why, if they were behaving in the classroom, they would be trusted to do the right thing with other students or in other parts of the school. The aim was to build capacity in the students to have all of them move out of the Ls category (in fact, they were going to have a pizza party when this happened), and thus build their independence and positive behaviour in the classroom.

Task completion in a flexible learning context

It is fascinating being in a role where I get to visit a range of different educational contexts – although they share many similarities, every context is unique and has creative ways to meet the needs of its learners.

In a flexible learning context that I visited, I was shown an example of student data on classroom walls of the that I thought was an important inclusion here. While it is to do with learning and task completion, it speaks more to keeping students on track and progressing than it does the 'quality of learning' aspect we'll discuss in the final five chapters of this part of the book.

In this school the young people have complex backgrounds, and the teachers work with them in a way that is trauma-informed and very responsive to their needs. On enrolment, each young person meets with a member of staff to identify goals for their time at the site, and teachers then deliberately break down successful completion in subjects, learning areas and other competencies into small, manageable chunks. They do this so that students can clearly see what they need to do next, but also to create small achievements and touchpoints for students to visibly see their progress and success.

The initial plan on entry to the school is recorded in goal-setting forms that are completed and stored in the young person's file. To make these goals and the tasks visible, however, the teachers have created a display in the classroom, showing the tasks each young person needs to complete. As shown in figure 24, teachers write the components requiring completion in a box relating to each subject. When a young person successfully completes the element, they both go to the wall and 'tick off' the component, and then cross out and write 'done' when the entire module is completed.

The teachers in the centre reported that they like this set-up, because the young people can clearly see what they need to do next (remembering they are co-constructed goals and plans); teachers can see where each learner is at quickly and easily; and if a young person has not attended for a while (this could be a few days up to a few weeks), they can quickly see where they were at and what they need to focus on.

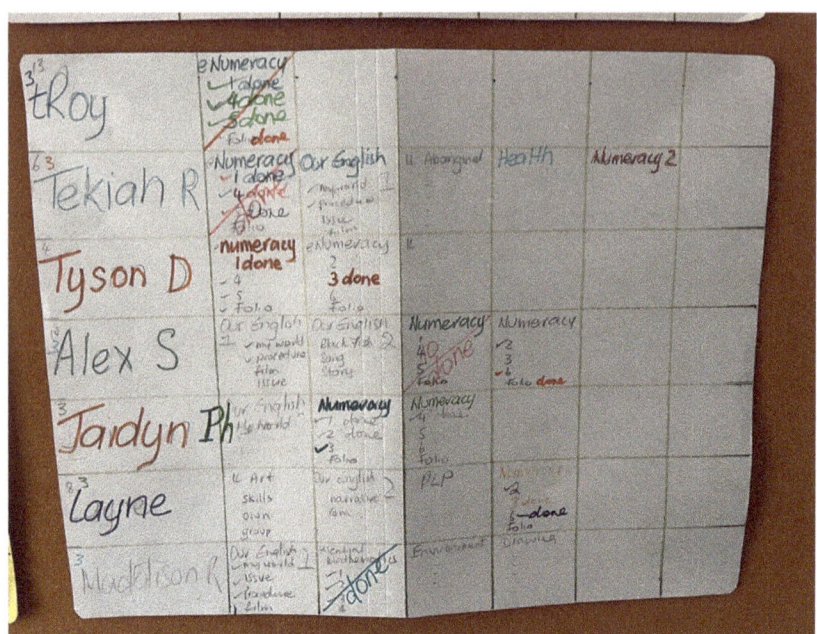

Figure 24: Task completion on the classroom wall in a flexible learning context

All the young people at this site are on individual learning plans and there is no explicit group teaching, meaning that the students choose what to work on at any given time. If they don't feel like completing the next literacy task, but there are tasks to do in art or numeracy, they can do these instead. The Head of Campus reported that it is the most effective system for them: they know that their young people are progressing, and everyone is always aware of where they are at with their learning.

Chapter 15

Intersection K: Quality of learning and data walls

Like intersections A and F, data walls showing the quality of learning that are not in the classroom are not used as extensively with students. However, there are a couple of examples that I have seen where they have been used to recognise and support student learning.

Reading growth awards

I have worked alongside a small regional primary school for a number of years. In late 2020, there was a window of lockdown freedom where I managed to travel to the school to do a day's work in person, which was a pleasant change given the pandemic and border restrictions across Australia. The focus of the day was on considering student progress, and looking for ways that learning growth and progress could be highlighted given the disruptions and challenges of the year.

One of the assessments that the school had to complete for reporting to its system was the Diagnostic Reading Assessment (DRA), where students are positioned on a reading level. The system required the school to assess students at the beginning and end of the year. There were system expectations and goals related to the expected reading level and student growth, according to the grade they were enrolled in at the school.

The challenge for this particular school was that students often entered the school with very low literacy levels, and teachers were often trying to bridge the gap and increase skill as quickly as they could, to minimise the level of disadvantage. Consequently, many students did not reach the year-level benchmarks, despite the best intentions, targeted and specific teaching, and pleasing growth and improvement in reading.

When I visited the school in late 2020, teachers and students had just completed their second set of reading assessments for the year. Teachers had placed the student data cards on the data wall in the staffroom – showing students who had and had not reached the associated benchmarks. I could tell that the teachers were disheartened and exhausted (given the challenging year they'd had), so I suggested changing the focus of the data wall to reflect the progress made, rather than whether or not students hit their benchmarks.

We took the cards off the wall and I made some changes to the categories, headings and positions of ribbons. I asked teachers to identify how many levels each student had progressed during the year, and to put them in an order from students who made the most progress to those who made the least. I then asked them to position the cards on the data wall based on the movement from the beginning to end of the year. Students who moved three or more reading levels were positioned at the top of the data wall; students who moved one or two levels were positioned in the middle of the data wall; and students who had not yet moved (or had not been retested) were in the lower section. As teachers put the individual student cards up in their new places and stepped back to look at the (very top-heavy) visualisation of the progress students had made (shown in figure 25), there was literally an audible sigh of relief.

Figure 25: Data wall in the staffroom showing student progress in reading

The teachers stood back and looked at the spread of students, and reflected that the data wall made them feel much better about the job they had done. Their impact on their students was immediately visible and very clear. It was probably one of the most powerful moments I've had as a data storyteller!

This was a long-winded way of getting to the point of this exercise – this data wall of student progress and growth, rather than achievement, made teachers feel professionally affirmed about the job they had done, as they could visibly see that most students had progressed, despite the year's challenges. The conversation that we had shifted and teachers talked about the improvements, and the students who had improved the most. Most importantly, this visualisation of the same data in a different way shifted the conversations that teachers had with their students. They were able to use what they had learned and seen on the data wall with students to highlight the good work that had been taking place.

As an extension of this, the school awarded the 'top five improvers' in reading (and also in numeracy – from a standardised numeracy assessment) at assembly. The Principal talked about learning being challenging and taking time, but that the students who were being recognised had worked hard and persisted. The teachers also reflected that there were several students recognised at assembly that day who do not ordinarily receive awards relating to their academic performance and achievement. It was a great exercise for all involved.

Two years later, at the end of 2022, I went back to the school to work with them in person again. The teachers remembered the work we did that day on progress and talked about it with fondness. What an absolute highlight!

Learner profile dashboards

In intersection A I shared the example of my nephew Jhye and his mentor having conversations about goal setting based on his electronic learner profile. While they are not the same as a traditional data wall that is built in a staff area, these platforms enable a student to log in and see their individual academic performance over time and across subject areas.

I worked in a school in Brisbane where they rolled out a student dashboard for all secondary students. Despite the fact that the rollout was the first time that students had been able to access their data in this way, the data had been entered for years, so students were able to see all their results from when they first enrolled in the school.

While this way of engaging students in a data conversation is not a traditional data wall as such, it is an increasingly useful tool that allows students to receive feedback on how they are performing. It is worth noting that the most common information that goes into these dashboards is summative assessment, which is problematic in terms of giving feedback because students don't ever really do the exact same task again; this makes it hard for students to know what they need to do next. However, if students are able to synthesise learnings across subject areas and assessment types (or, fingers crossed, tech companies work out how to make formative and summative results visible in the same spot), students can zoom out and think about the broader feedback and gaps in their work.

Often these visualisation dashboards compare performance in a particular subject area over time, so the student can see a line graph, for example, that shows their longitudinal performance in English, and the trend of their result over time. This can be really useful for them, and it also helps build their capacity to read, understand and interpret this information.

Part of the effective use of these dashboards is teaching students about the data and building their data literacy. As adults who mark student work, we know that if a student gets a B in English, the B is a single global result that is the culmination of a whole lot of data points underneath. To generate a B grade overall, there would be overall results for individual tasks, which have results for each individual criterion; even within each criterion, there are elements and descriptors that the student will or will not have achieved. While these global results can be really useful, we need to remind students that the data does not tell them what to do with the information, or where specifically they can improve – it just gives them an overall understanding of their performance.

Many of these learning management systems also show student performance in standardised assessment; for example, they might show a young person's performance in the standardised literacy and numeracy assessments across a range of tests. The dashboards that do this well show the results of each test, and some compare the student's performance against their school cohort or national averages. Others, such as general ability assessments, are sometimes mapped against school results – for example, GPA versus general ability result.

I believe in the power of sharing these dashboards with students – as it can provide useful, tangible and often more objective comparisons. At the same time, I also am very conscious that training and support for students in using this data needs to be a priority. If a young person looks at their dashboard for the first time without any preparation and sees a disappointing result, they probably will not react well, and they may disengage from the tool completely.

In chapter 4 I provided some ideas as to how you might choose to start conversations with students when they first see their learning data in this way. As the adults in the room, it is important to acknowledge to students that we know that people have different strengths; that the assessments we use in schools do not assess every aspect of a person; and that they do not, in fact, assess things that matter such as creativity, teamwork and loyalty. Normalising this, and promoting the benefits of having a good understanding of where we are at, is an important part of any use of data in this way.

In my experience of seeing this type of data visualisation being provided to students I have noticed, more than any other concerns, staff fear: fear about doing it 'right', setting students up for success and anticipating future confrontation. I am often asked questions about what might happen if a student logs on and finds out they are at the bottom of their cohort or their class. While I am very aware of students such as these, at the same time, I would say that those young people are usually very aware of where they are already, so it wouldn't necessarily come as a surprise to them.

Another question I am often asked is about parents/guardians – what if the parent sees a trend that they are not happy with? Will it come back on the school? While it might be the first time a parent sees data on student performance mapped semester to semester, as analytics legend Andrew Webb reminded me, they have had access to all of this data before the dashboard rollout. Subject reports, assessment results and standardised assessment results generally all make their way home to parents via different reports at different times. The dashboard just puts it in a user-friendly interface where they see the data visualised in a different way.

There is one caveat that is worth adding to this conversation, and that is about the importance of having processes that check in on students and their dashboard usage. While we would like to think that students will engage in the process and use the tool, not all students will. Possibly of more interest, though, are students who log on too often and become fixated on checking their results. In one of the schools I was involved with, there was a student who, we realised, had logged in to check his results 40 times in the first few weeks of having dashboard access. This was in the early part of the term; given that summative assessment results were only released and visible after marking, moderation and middle leader release, it did not make sense for this student to log in as frequently as he was. This information was passed on to a teacher who worked with him regularly, who had a conversation with him about how the dashboard worked. It turned out that there was a complete misconception – the student thought it would continue to be updated regularly, and did not realise that only key data sets would show on the dashboard. The teacher talked through when he might expect results to show, and the number of logins dropped immediately. The student went on to use the tool at the appropriate times. It is worth pointing out that if you intend to roll out a program such as this, it is important to think about how you manage expectations and ensure healthy use of the tool.

Chapter 16

Intersection L: Quality of learning and using success criteria

There is a lot written about the importance of learning intentions and success criteria. The added step of co-constructing success criteria with students can have a significant impact, as it is a time for students to engage in considering themselves as learners. Co-creation is beneficial because it helps students understand what learning looks like, what is expected of them and what they need to do to progress.

Co-constructing success criteria would not happen all the time, and it would (quite frankly) be a waste of time for short bursts of content or skill that you are not working on over an extended period. However, in times where you are working on something consistently, over a couple of weeks or a unit, it can be an incredibly useful tool.

Quality of learning and feedback – senior mock exam

One way of using data with students and reporting on the quality of their work is through specific and targeted feedback on practice or mock exams. This looks different in every school, and it varies based on the year level.

Traditionally (and without the use of technology) we used to mark a practice exam, provide feedback and return the task to the student. These assessments were ether quite similar to what a student might expect to see in the final exam, or (in the case of the final year of schooling) a past paper that a previous cohort was given.

One of the ways that technology can help teachers provide specific and targeted feedback to students is through automation – not of the marking itself, but for grouping data, assigning feedback and suggesting areas for improvement.

In the first example I saw of this, the teacher marked the hard copy of the paper and allocated the required marks to each question. They entered each student's results, for each question, onto a central spreadsheet. This data fed into a different tab or spreadsheet for each student in the cohort, which produced a personalised visualisation of their results.

On this page, the student could see not only the questions they got wrong but also the sections of the paper that they struggled with the most, and the areas of the syllabus that most needed their attention. In spreadsheet set-up, each question had been attached to a specific element and subsection of the syllabus, so the spreadsheet aggregated the results for each component (see the right-hand side of figure 26). It highlighted all the syllabus sections and subsections where the student achieved less than 50 per cent of the available marks (in a cream background with red text), and it prioritised the areas that the student should address first.

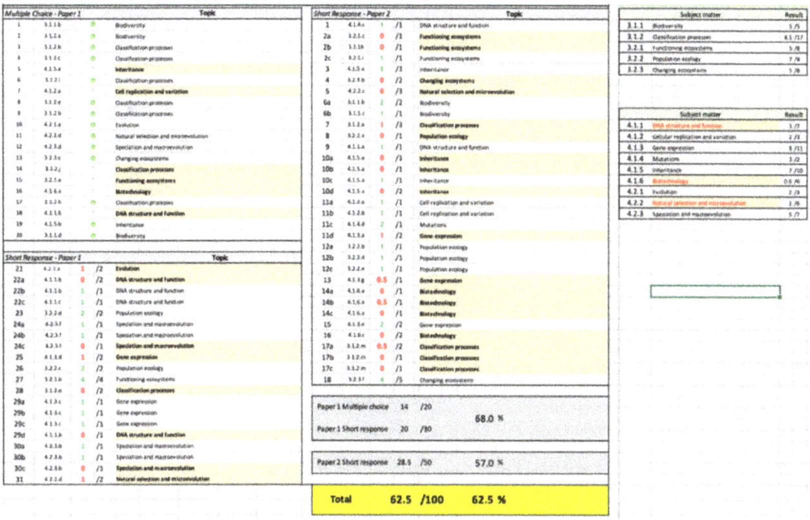

Figure 26: Example summary of mock exam results, including the syllabus areas requiring most attention

Recently I saw a similar version of this tracking in another school that was doing the same types of calculation and feedback around areas of the syllabus that needed attention. It went one step further and provided, for each of the incorrect questions in the mock exam, specific questions and exercises for the student to practise. Rather than students needing to ascertain how to practise the skills or learn the content they needed to, the program did the thinking for the student, automatically providing a list of activities for them to complete.

The interesting thing about this process was that teachers were almost completely removed from the feedback experience. Of course, students could speak with teachers about their results if they wanted to; but the use of automation technology meant that students had clear direction about what they needed to do to improve, without the teacher's input. It was also set up so that the student's results on the practice exam, and their identified strengths and gaps, generated a 'comment' for teachers to provide written feedback to students and parents. In this feedback, the questions and sections that were recommended to the student were listed.

When I spoke with students about how they had used the tool, and how they were progressing towards the final external exam, they could tell me specifically which areas they were struggling with; which areas they were confident in; and exactly what they needed to do to try to improve their results. The beauty of this approach was in the automation – the teacher did not have to handle every student's individual questions and data to provide specific feedback about what they should focus on next. Yet the feedback was incredibly targeted and specific for the students.

The other thing that I really liked about both examples was that they used technology the school already had access to, such as Microsoft Excel or Google Forms. While they do rely on having a member of staff (or a teaching team) who is technologically savvy and can produce this for you, teachers have reported that the time investment is worth the return, and saves them a lot of time when students complete mock exams. This is particularly important in departments, or for teachers, who teach multiple senior subjects. Although it is time-consuming to set up, and a different version is required for each practice exam, the spreadsheet can be reused each time you have a different cohort of students complete that same mock exam.

Tracking competencies in a certificate course

In intersection G I shared the example of Greg, the teacher who thought he did not collect any data but actually kept clear records of learner attributes in a spreadsheet for his vocational subject.

It probably will not surprise you to know that Greg also used a comprehensive tracking method for completion of competencies. Unlike the previous example that identified gaps only, this tracking provided information to students on the competencies they had completed to date, showing clear expectations about what they needed to do next.

As shown in figure 27, Greg was undertaking this process for the Certificate II in Engineering Pathways. The success criteria were divided into 20 elements across the two years, including 'toolbox', 'own design', 'career plan' and 'mass production'. When the student demonstrated an element of the competency and Greg had adequate evidence of completion, he recorded the element as completed. Greg filled in boxes over time, ultimately getting to the point of placing 'yes' automatically in the final two columns as students completed each element, then the course overall.

While this was a teacher record stored on his own computer, Greg regularly used this with students and parents to discuss the progress students were making and the areas that were complete (or missing). Greg reported that students would often ask to view their page to see what they next needed to do; and that it was a good way for students to track their own performance and set goals about what they would be working on next.

If a student was falling behind in their completion of the elements or the competencies, Greg said that this was a useful way of providing specific information to students about where they were at and what they needed to do to catch up. Certificate courses require good record-keeping and evidence of competencies, but the way Greg used this data with students made it an important inclusion here. The best part about all of this was breaking it to Greg that he did, in fact, collect a lot of data, and had been for the last 15 years!

MEM20413 - Certificate II in Engineering Pathways

Name: | Started: | Certificate II Achieved: **YES** | Assessor: **GPN** | 41

Homeroom: | Completed: | Withdrawn from Course:

MEM20413 Certificate II in Engineering Pathways		Assessment Items	1 Safety Exercise 1	2 Toolbox	3 Environmental Issues 1	4 MMAW Exercise 1 & 2	5 Aluminium Hammer	6 Career Report 1	7 The "L"	8 MMAW Project	9 Aluminium Dice	10 Mass Production 1	11 Own Design 1	12 Safety Exercise 2	13 Environmental Issues 2	14 Chipping Hammer	15 GMAW Exercises 1 & 2	16 GMAW Project	17 Career Plan	18 The "T"	19 Mass Production 2	20 Own Design 2	Elements Achieved	Competency Achieved	Blank Cells	Elements	Element Points
			Year One											Year Two													
Competencies	Elements		2	8	#8	3	3	#4	3	3	3	7	8	#1	#6	3	3	3	#4	3	8	10					
MEM 13014A Apply OH&S in the workplace	Follow safe working practices		X	X			X											X				X	Yes	Yes	15	1	3
	Report workplace accidents		X	X			X											X				X	Yes		15	1	
	Follow emergency procedures		X	X			X											X				X	Yes		15	1	
MEM 16006A Organise and communicate information	Access information		X									X	X	X					X			X	Yes	Yes	14	1	3
	Organise & analyse information		X									X	X	X					X			X	Yes		14	1	
	Communicate information		X									X	X	X					X			X	Yes		14	1	
MEM 16008A Interact with computing technology	Determine job requirements		X										X	X									Yes	Yes	17	1	5
	Access information/data		X										X	X									Yes		17	1	
	Input information/data		X										X	X									Yes		17	1	
	Store information/data		X										X	X									Yes		17	1	
	Access assistance as required		X										X	X									Yes		17	1	
MEM 18001C	Use hand tools			X					X											X			Yes	Yes	17	1	1
MEM 18002B	Use hand held power tools			X		X							X					X				X	Yes	Yes	15	1	1
	Prepare a job plan						X				X					X						X	Yes		16	1	

Figure 27: Spreadsheet that tracked student competencies

Assessment and learning checklists

Another way of using success criteria to help students understand what learning and success looks like is to provide checklists. When I taught senior Physical Education and students had to complete a theory task, we would often detail the elements of success in a checklist so they could work through the list and ensure they had covered specific elements.

For example, in an assignment on biomechanics, some of the success criteria that appeared in the checklist were:

- the need for concise and clear communication
- 'big ideas' that should appear at some stage in the response
- keywords and specific content that should be included
- specific cognitions or thinking skills that should occur (for example, an analysis of the technique in the video and evaluation of its effectiveness)

- levels and expectations relating to referencing (specifically the number of sources and the types of sources that needed to be included).

The teaching team found these checklists were often more useful for students than having a conversation about the quality of their work relative to the marking rubric. Rubrics are often written in teacher-centric language, and students often find it difficult to ascertain the differences between levels (for example, the difference between a 'discerning analysis' and a 'detailed analysis'). They did, however, engage in conversations about the components of the task, how they were meeting the expectations in the checklist and what they needed to do to improve their written response. We also found that, rather than setting a broad assessment task or matrix that students struggled to unpack, the checklist gave more detail and clarity about what was expected of them.

Traffic light self-reflection

When I was visiting a school recently, one of the middle leaders, Carly, shared with me the way that her students self-reflect on their knowledge and skill based on clearly defined success criteria.

Carly's teaching team developed the success criteria shown in figure 28, and all year-level teachers shared this document with students at the beginning of the unit. As the unit progressed, students were encouraged to reflect on what they had learned and what their level of skill and understanding was. The document outlined what students would be learning throughout the unit and it provided, in student-centred language, details about what students should be able to do by the end of the unit. Students were asked to tick the colour corresponding to their level of skill and understanding: green for good/confident, yellow for satisfactory/still need to do some work, and red for finding it hard/need to really practise.

Climate Graphs	I know what a climate graph is and how to build one.	🟢	🟡	🔴

Statistics	I know how to identify and interpret different types of statistics:
	   o Pie graphs
	   o Line graphs
	   o Column graphs
	   o Proportional graphs
	   o Data conversion
		🟢	🟡	🔴

Synoptic Charts (Weather Maps)	I know how to identify the different symbols of a synoptic chart and interpret current weather conditions.	🟢	🟡	🔴

Map Types	I can identify and interpret different features on the following map types:
	   o Thematic
	   o Choropleth
	   o Topographic
	   o Political
	   o Cartograms
		🟢	🟡	🔴

Latitude and Longitude	I can identify Australia on a world map and name states, cities, and surrounding oceans.	🟢	🟡	🔴
	I can label the continents and oceans of the world.	🟢	🟡	🔴
	I know how to use an atlas.	🟢	🟡	🔴
Annotation	I know how to label and annotate a photograph and diagram.	🟢	🟡	🔴

Figure 28: A section of a traffic light self-assessment tool for Geography

If students completed an exam at the end of the unit, this tool was used as an opportunity for students to reflect on what they had learned prior to the exam to direct their revision. Students could see the areas that they struggled with the most (in red) and they might choose to invest time in these areas first. They would also be able to see the areas that they were most comfortable with (green) which would still require revision, but potentially not as much. While the 'data' was categorical, rather than numerical, it provided a good opportunity for students to be engaged in their learning and data story.

Chapter 17

Intersection M: Quality of learning and using student-generated assessment

In intersection C we looked at the way student-generated assessment can be used to support students to set goals, know their goals and take steps towards achievement. There is a little overlap between intersection C and intersection M, but the examples provided here focus more on the quality of the response, rather than on setting and achieving goals.

Science folio example

I worked with a Head of Science who wanted to try student-generated assessment in their subject area and classroom, but was not sure how to do so, or what it might look like. In Science, there is a lot of content knowledge that is important (and needs to be assessed), and there are a number of skills that also need to be demonstrated and assessed. The middle leader wanted to rethink the way that they assessed student knowledge and skill, and decided that student-generated assessment outside of set exams or assignment tasks was how they wanted to progress. (Just a note: this is different to the previous example with Kev as that was a set folio. This was a different leader who wanted to involve students in the process of deciding how they would be assessed.)

Consequently, they implemented a folio for the term. They shared the learning objectives of the unit, the parts of the achievement standard and elaborations that they were focusing on, and they spoke with students about it being their job, throughout the term, to find and provide evidence of their learning and skill to meet the criteria. Students were provided with documentation that showed what they needed to demonstrate, and some potential ways of showing this learning, and were tasked with submitting eight folio pieces throughout the term to demonstrate different elements.

Students were stepped through the process (obviously they could not have done this well, the first time, with little guidance). They were encouraged to think about how they could demonstrate their knowledge, and they had flexibility in what that looked like in the folio. Students completed inquiry questions, graphed and analysed experiment results, visualised the layers of rocks and annotated drawings, interviewed one another, and wrote mini-essays about the movement of tectonic plates in different parts of the world.

The Head of Science marked the work against the criteria each time students submitted a piece, and students had a running record of where they were at with different elements of the course. The great thing about this process was that if students were not happy with the 'grade' they were given for each component, they were allowed to submit more (or different) evidence to increase their grade. There were times they had demonstrated a superficial understanding of the topic, so went back, learned more and were able to talk in more detail about the concept. At other times, they had made mistakes in their work, and they had the opportunity to go back and fix their work and resubmit it.

This process undoubtedly meant an ongoing cycle of marking student work, tracking and updating results, and keeping good records of student results. However, the Head of Science reported that students were more invested in this assessment because it did not rely on students performing solely in an end-of-term exam; they had a lot of autonomy around the way that they would be assessed; and they had the option to improve their result if they were not happy with it.

Year 11 and 12 Physics matrix

Just to keep you on your toes, I'm going to throw in an example here from the 1990s.

One of the subjects that I studied in my final years of schooling was Physics. The fact that I spent most of those lessons sitting beside the oval watching the Physical Education lessons 'doing my Physics work' rather than being in the classroom is sort of irrelevant at this point – but is funny, nonetheless.

My Physics teacher at the time, Mr Larsen, was completing his doctorate. My understanding was that the way he structured our senior assessment was something that he was researching. Assessment in Mr Larsen's class was unique; we had a matrix of assessment tasks throughout the course. Different tasks were in different modes, assessed different elements of the curriculum and demonstrated different skills and understanding. Each time we completed a task and had our result and feedback returned to us, we would take out our profile sheet that was at the front of our folio and fill in the appropriate section.

Like in other subject areas, we would reflect on how we had gone; we would (in my case) commit to working harder next time; and we would think about future assessment and how it was similar and different to the task we had just completed. The interesting element in this class, however, was that we also got to 'cross out' tasks where we had lower scores, if they were able to be replaced by assessment tasks with higher scores.

While this was a couple of decades ago, I remember the parameters that were set – we needed to have a certain number of assessment tasks completed; we needed to have covered off all the curriculum elements for the course; and we could only 'cross something out' if there was a comparable task to replace it with. We were well versed in the fact that there could not be gaps in our profile – we were playing the game, if you like, but with some clear parameters about what we could and could not do.

What it meant for me, as a learner, was that I had agency over the way my final grades and results would be calculated. I could choose to invest a lot of time and effort in a particular task in the hope that I would get a better result than a previous piece, knowing which lower result I could potentially remove. I did not feel as though assessment was something that was being 'done to me' and that I could not control; I felt I was completely in control, and it was great. There were limitations, obviously. There were results that I could not remove that I would have liked to, but because we were not covering the topic or skill again, I would not get a chance to improve my grade; however, if anything, the approach motivated me to influence the tasks that I could.

There were lots of innovative things that happened in my secondary school, but Mr Larsen absolutely deserves a shout out for his work in this space (and for letting me 'work' beside the oval).

Chapter 18

Intersection N: Quality of learning and deliberate conversations

Having deliberate conversations about the quality of learning or level of understanding is probably the intersection that we do most frequently, and are most comfortable with as teachers. We are often having conversations with students individually about their learning, where they are at and what they need to do to improve. It is also relatively common for teachers to talk to entire classes or cohorts about how they are progressing, raising any persistent concerns or celebrating good results.

The examples in this section, therefore, will not be significantly new or different to things that you probably already do. However, they are included here to show some examples of different options we have and ways that other teachers do things.

Conversations about formative writing tasks

Legendary human and teacher, Annalea, shared the following example with me, describing the way she used data in conversations with her students to improve their writing. This approach has worked in mainstream English lessons across Years 7 to 12, but also for students for whom English is an additional language or dialect, and for beginning English speakers. Annalea explained that depending on where students were up to in their writing, they could focus on developing vocabulary and simple sentences, through to complex sentences, paragraphing, building complexity and using literary devices.

When Annalea started this process, she began by using a rubric for writing that came from a standardised, nation-wide writing assessment. She used these 'levels' alongside grammar resources to develop a plan for explicit goals and progress tracking. In the lessons students would complete a 'quick write' session, following some explicit teaching (for example, on syntax, grammar, connectives, literacy devices, modelled genre pieces and so on). The quick writes and explicit teaching of writing was used by Annalea to begin every lesson for students in Years 7 to 10, and once per week for Year 11 and 12 students if their writing proficiency was at standard. Annalea also sat with students individually (usually once a fortnight) to review goals, support their learning or extend their skill.

Each fortnight, Annalea would collect the writing samples, provide feedback and work with students to set a goal for the following two weeks. If there were similarities and consistencies across students' writing, she would use that as an explicit teaching opportunity for the whole class, or for a small group in the class. Prior to the quick write, Annalea would remind students of their individual goals, and talked through their specific feedback and teaching points. The data goals were also on the classroom wall, and when students achieved them they were celebrated.

Annalea said that it was useful not only for conversations with students in the classroom, but also with parents/guardians, as she was able to talk specifically about the elements of writing that had improved and the next steps for the student.

Tracking student achievement in summative tasks

While I was writing this book, high school teacher Jo-Anne reached out to me to share the way she uses data with students in her senior Business subject. Given that this subject contributes to students' tertiary entrance rank, the level of learning and understanding of the subject content and skills is particularly important for students wanting to be successful.

Jo-Anne tracks student results not only in the overall score that students achieve for each task, but in each criterion or cognition, as well as the subsections of each. Each criterion contains three characteristics for the highest band, so rather than only tracking the number of marks students achieve, Jo-Anne also tracks how well students have satisfied the characteristics in the criterion.

As shown in figure 29, each criterion is allocated three columns in a spreadsheet, to represent the three characteristics within each mark band of the criterion. Each row represents one student, and Jo-Anne colour-codes the cells for each descriptor as either:

- green – meets the top mark
- orange – one below the top mark
- red – two or more below the top mark.

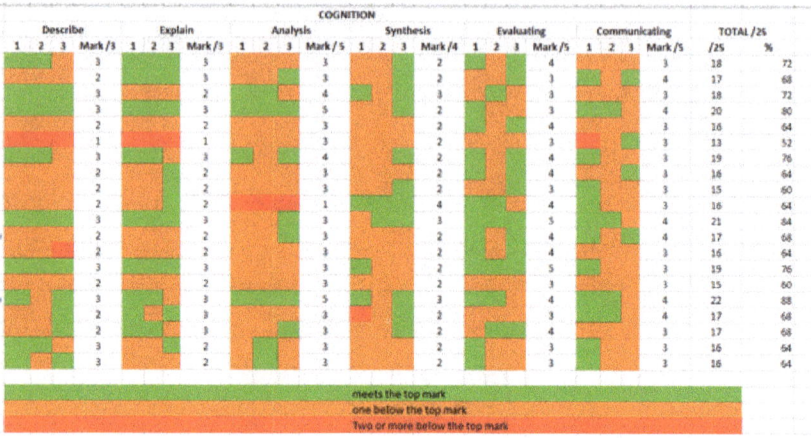

Figure 29: Class spreadsheet for an assessment task, broken down to criterion and characteristic

Collecting and collating the data in this way allows Jo-Anne to see the proportion of red, orange and green across the tasks, cognitions that might be higher or lower than others, students who are doing particularly well and those who are not, and specific areas for students and the class to work on.

This information is not often shared with students in a collective way (when it is, it is de-identified); instead, students see their row only in their online notebook, with detailed evaluative and coaching feedback (as shown in figure 30).

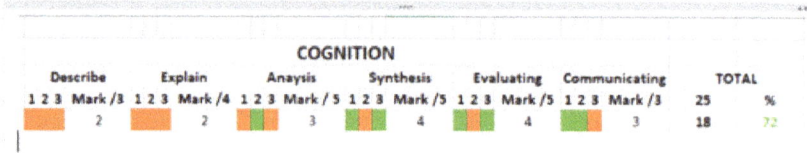

Figure 30: The individual version seen by students

Jo-Anne showed that as the course progresses, students build a bank of results and visualisations (as depicted in figure 30) and detailed written feedback. As the assessment in the first year of the course is largely replicated in the second year, this feedback provides information to students about not only what they did and what could have been improved in the task they finished, but also clear guidance on how to approach the task and things to be mindful of in the second year. This individualised data and feedback provides useful information for conversations in the classroom about performance and goal setting. Jo-Anne has regular conversations with students about these results and talks with each student about how they can improve.

Individual conferencing

When I was undertaking research for my thesis, I was fortunate to be able to interview students and teachers from three secondary schools about their perceptions of feedback. It was an incredible privilege to learn about the ways that other teachers work. This research into feedback was the first time that I had heard about formalised individual conferencing with students, and I have since seen and heard about countless examples of this practice. While we often have conversations with students about the quality of their work, the notion of conferencing that I discuss here relates to the formalised process. In these instances, it is often undertaken as a feedback strategy, generally on drafts of summative assessment tasks.

In this particular example, the school ran formalised assessment conferencing for students across the school, but it was particularly prevalent in the Science department. After students submitted their drafts and teachers marked them, teachers would allocate a couple of lessons in which to return the feedback to students through individual conferencing. They allocated a small amount of time (three minutes, for example) for students to discuss their draft and feedback with the teacher. The teacher highlighted gaps in the work and areas the student should focus on, and would talk through next steps prior to submission of the final assessment.

The main criticism that I heard from students in this school was that some teachers did not allow students to voice record the session, and therefore students had to remember all the comments and/or write notes on what the teacher was saying. Some students said they felt there was a lot of pressure on them to remember everything, and inevitably they didn't, meaning there was a lot of feedback that they missed.

I have seen this practice run in other settings, with different variations to the conditions or the way it is run. For example:

- some teachers allow voice recording of the feedback so students can review what was said.
- modifications are made to the time allocated. This is largely dependent on class size. I have heard of some conferencing sessions being as short as two minutes and others as long as 10 minutes per student.
- in some instances, this process can be run as a 'cold' exercise for the teacher, where the student brings a particular section of their work, rather than the whole assignment) to the conference and seeks feedback on the element of the task. For example, the student might bring the first body paragraph, or the first 200 words of a story. The teacher reads and responds to the part of the task in the moment, rather than doing any pre-work or marking.

The examples above relate, usually, to summative assessment tasks; however, this does not always have to be the case. Formalised conferencing can be used on formative activities or other class activities as well, and this approach can be used for individual conversations or with groups of students working together.

Like with all feedback strategies, there are pros and cons to this approach, and it will not suit every teacher or every student. But it can be a useful way of providing similar amounts of feedback to students if that is an issue, and also an opportunity for a formalised one-on-one conversation with the student about the quality of their work.

Sharing class results in summative assessment

Providing students with group feedback about their performance on assessment tasks is another way we can have deliberate conversations with students about their performance. As teachers, making overall and summary comments about how students have performed is part and parcel of what we do. Again, the difference here is in the inclusion of specific student data in the conversation to provide evidence to inform students.

I have seen this unfold in several ways, and this is just one example. In my first book, *Using and Analysing Data in Australian Schools*, I provided an example of a writing task for Year 8 students – and that example could have very easily fit here, too. In this instance, however, the teacher of a Year 12 class wanted to provide summary information to students about their results in internal assessments and their mock exam for their external exam.

The teacher developed the visualisation shown in figure 31, to represent the class's average result in internal assessment 1, internal assessment 3 and the external exam mock exam. The teacher chose to exclude internal assessment 2 from the visualisation as it was a very different type of task compared with these three similar tasks.

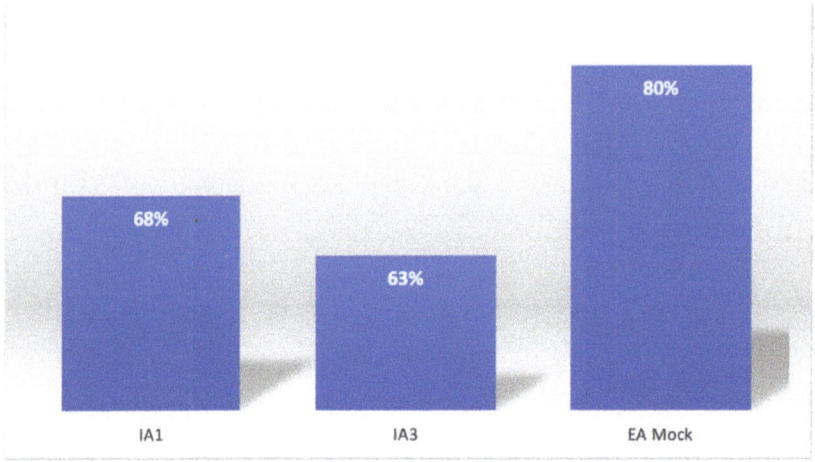

Figure 31: Tracking overall class average results in different assessment tasks

She facilitated a conversation about the differences between the tasks, highlighting the strength in their preparation for the external exam, and the improvements they had made from the internal assessment tasks. The class discussed the drop in average results in internal assessment 3, and they talked about the factors that had impacted these results. This conversation led to a discussion about ways to support one another, and how they could work together to build on their success from the mock exam.

The teacher then had individual conversations with students about their performance in the assessment tasks. Using figure 32, she showed students their results in different tasks, and had a goal-setting conversation with students about what they intended to do next.

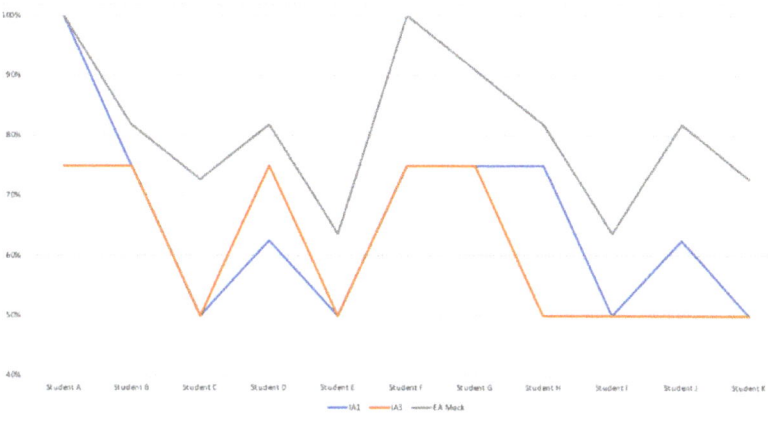

Figure 32: Tracking student performance in individual tasks over time

As shown in figure 32, two students achieved 100 per cent on the mock exam and no student achieved below 60 per cent, but the conversations were quite different, particularly considering the results that they had 'banked' in previous assessment tasks.

The teacher said that the combination of class-level and individual conversations worked well. She said that students appreciated the chance to have specific conversations about their results, and to see them visualised in a different way. The group conversation opened up the discussion; however, we also know that average results lack the detail that pertains to individual students. Therefore, the individual conversations allowed for the nuance and specific detail that the class-level conversation lacked.

Chapter 19

Intersection O: Quality of learning and data on walls

The final intersection is about the quality of learning or understanding, and using data on classroom walls to highlight this. Again, some of these examples might easily have appeared in other sections, but they are particularly valid here.

Levels of understanding on a classroom wall

An example that I have seen on classroom walls, related to the quality of learning or level of understanding, is where teachers have 'levels' describing a student's understanding, and students self-assess and place their name on the associated level. There are two main ways that I have seen this done: with the equivalent of a proficiency scale (or something that unpacks and describes levels of understanding in the specific unit), or generic levels of understanding that could be used across units and topics.

In the first instance, the teacher has different levels of descriptors that relate to the particular unit of work or skill that the class is learning. There are usually five levels, with the first being a descriptor that says students need help to be able to perform the task or do the work, through to high-level cognitions about the depth of understanding and ability to apply and transfer the information to different contexts. This strategy is useful as it unpacks clearly what the specific levels of learning look like, but it is time-consuming in that the descriptors need to be developed for each unit or task the teacher would like to use this strategy with.

The other option is to have a generic set of levels that remain on the wall for extended periods, with the first level being that students need assistance to complete the work, through to the highest level being that students can teach and support other students. There are plenty of versions for different visuals and levels available online, so the teacher can choose a theme that suits the interests of students in class (some examples include showing the number of fingers, ice-cream scoops or basketball skills). This generic version is beneficial as teachers can keep it on their wall for an extended period and use the levels across different subject areas; and students can develop a thorough understanding of what the levels mean, making the process quick and easy each time the teacher wants to use it.

There are a number of ways that students can self-reflect and position themselves on the levels, depending on teacher and learner preferences. In many instances, I have seen students with their own data card that they place on or around the level they are sitting at. These data cards have plenty of options, including:

- a picture of a student and their name
- a picture only
- a name only
- a made-up identifier – such as a superhero, an animal, a nickname, or a colour.

At other times (and like in the success criteria example earlier in part 3), I have seen teachers post a laminated page below the level and students have been able to write their name underneath.

Regardless of the strategy the teacher uses, students should be encouraged to move themselves up the levels as they deepen their understanding and skill.

Literacy clusters on a classroom wall

Recently I saw a classroom where the teacher printed all the literacy clusters that were used in her school, and students were positioned with de-identified 'bug' cards on the cluster that they were working at. The goal was for students to be able to demonstrate the skills and understanding outlined in Cluster 12 by the end of Year 6.

The teacher explained that when she first introduced this strategy, she explained to students the goal to have everyone at Cluster 12 by the end of the year, and she talked about how they would work together to build literacy skills as a team. The teacher talked with students about why this was important, and how literacy skills would be essential throughout their lives – not just in Year 6 (or in high school).

Following this introduction, she had targeted conversations with each student about where they were on the list of clusters. In these conversations she identified the areas they were doing well in, and the areas that were the next to focus on. Students wrote their goals and next steps in their books. Then, as shown in figure 33, they chose a name for their beetle, and put it on the wall beside the cluster they were working on.

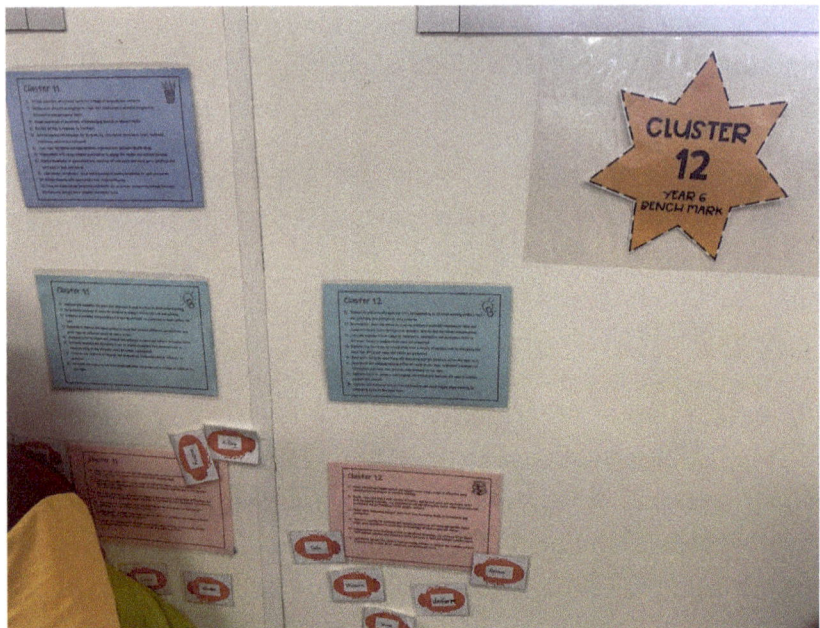

Figure 33: Current cluster performance

When I visited the classroom, students spoke to me about the level that they were on, and clearly and concisely explained the things that they could do already, and the things they were working on next. The teacher said that when they demonstrated the next skill, she would celebrate with them, tick it off their list, and they would talk about the next steps. When students moved up a cluster, she celebrated with them, and students proudly moved their beetle along the wall. The teacher said that although it took her some time to set up and help students understand how the wall would be used, it was worth the time investment, as students could talk very specifically about what their next steps were. When I spoke to students, it was clear that she had normalised that different students are at different stages at different times, and that we all have different strengths. This example was a real testament to her and the way she brought students along on the journey!

Writing process

As I was writing this book, I stumbled across the following example in a school that I was presenting in. I really liked the visibility of the process, but also that this was not a 'race' – it was an ongoing cycle, where students, when they finished a piece of writing, went back to the beginning and started again with their next piece.

The teacher in this Year 6 classroom displayed the following steps to follow in the process of writing:

1. planning
2. drafting
3. revising
4. editing
5. publishing.

She decided to use this resource on the classroom wall, to guide students through their independent writing sessions, helping them improve the quality of their writing. The teacher said that while there were times where students would write specific types of texts for different reasons, and that these are due at different times, in their independent writing time students were able to write with a lot of choice regarding genre, topic and length. Consequently, students engaged in the writing process cycle at their own pace, and cycled through the process for each independent piece of writing throughout the year.

As shown in figure 34, each student had a sticky note with their name on it, and as they progressed from one stage to the next they moved their sticky note. Each of the laminated pages had a description of what occurs at each stage, so that students could check in if they were unsure what they needed to do next. They progressed through the stages, refining and improving their work;

and when they had published their writing, they would return to the top and begin planning what they will write next. The teacher said it helped students remember the process and reminded them what to do next, and the open-ended nature of the task allowed students to write independently on what they were interested in at the time.

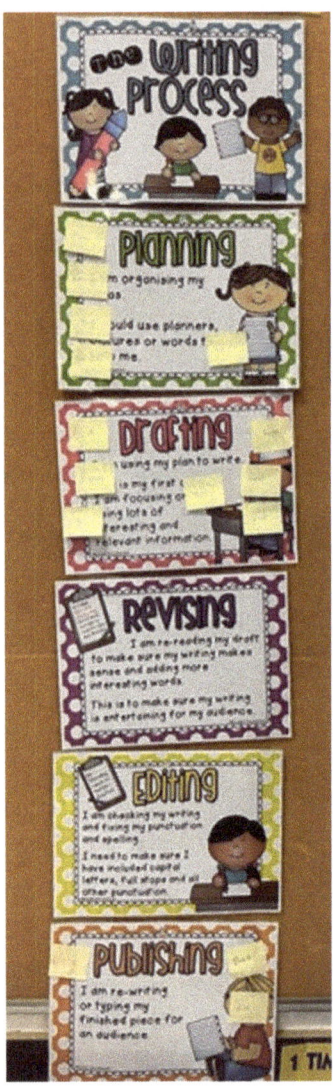

Figure 34: The steps of writing success, from planning to publishing

Part 3 has unpacked the 15 intersections of data-informed learners by considering the ways in which we provide information to students on goal setting, behaviour and learner dispositions, and the quality of learning and levels of understanding. These examples have sought to provide inspiration around the ways you could potentially approach this work with students, but also to provide prompts for you to create new, more effective and more contextually appropriate options for your classroom. Ultimately, the ins and outs of how you choose to engage students in their data story do not matter as much as your willingness and openness to involve them in the process.

Conclusion

As teachers, we aim to do everything we can to positively impact the students in our care. The best way we can do this is to act on the evidence that we have access to, using it to benefit our students and shift our practice. If we are able to collect reliable evidence of learning and act on this evidence, we can exist in the top right quadrant of figure 35, where we have a positive impact on our students. As demonstrated throughout this book, when we can engage and involve students in their data story, they become agents of their own learning and our impact is amplified.

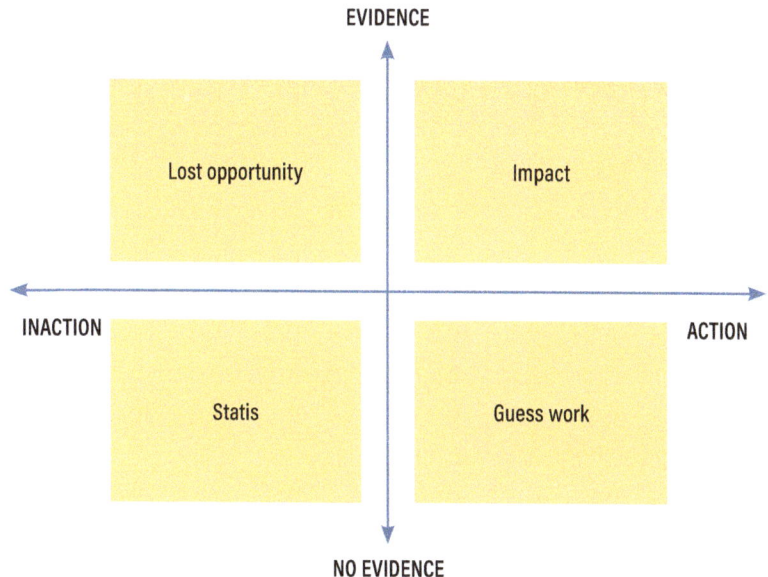

Figure 35: Evidence versus action quadrant (from Fisk 2022a)

Using data with students is done to varying degrees by different educators in different schools. While this notion is not new – many teachers have done this for decades – this book has hopefully provided some practical examples of ways this could be done in this relatively new landscape of data and learning analytics. I hope it has sparked inspiration for you, and that it gets you thinking about what might work for you, your students and your classroom. In the examples provided throughout part 3, it is clear that the notion of 'data' takes different forms – there are almost equal amounts of quantitative and qualitative examples in this book, and neither are more right or wrong than the other. They both have a place.

When we are thinking about using data with students, we do so for one of three reasons: quality of learning, behaviour or learner dispositions, and goal setting. We do so through different modes: data walls, success criteria, student-generated assessment, deliberate conversations and data on classroom walls. The power of this work is in the specific intersections of the purpose and mode; part 3 of this book unpacked a range of examples of how that could potentially look.

In the earlier part of this book, I also discussed the difference between progress and achievement data. Some of the examples provided in part 3 have highlighted opportunities to view and discuss progress for learners, not just their achievement. All the 15 intersections between purpose and mode could be used for progress or achievement methods, and I encourage you to think about the ways in which you could expand this thinking and the examples in this book to find more opportunities to do this for your students.

In the introduction, I suggested that students who are data-informed:

- have a deeper understanding of their strengths
- are able to articulate the specific areas they need to work on
- know the difference between their achievement and the progress they have made
- are more confident in talking about their progress and achievement
- have a better understanding of what is expected of them in the learning area or task
- are respectful of their peers' strengths and weaknesses and positively support others
- encourage other teachers to engage with them at the same level in the use of data.

Despite the discomfort you might feel in trialling new things with your students, lean into that discomfort (as Brené Brown says) and test the waters slowly. Just like when you were learning other data skills and beginning to have conversations with your colleagues about data, start small, and focus on the positives that you see. Like learning any new skill, it takes time to build confidence. Sometimes small steps feel the safest, but if you keep taking small steps forward, you will eventually get there. Your students will tell you everything you need to know about how these conversations assist them, and they will encourage you to expand your practice further.

We are living in a world that is data-informed; we are not data-driven, and we never want our students to be data-driven. It is our role to show them how being data-informed is human and imperfect, but can be incredibly powerful when they engage in their unique data story.

About the author

Selena is a data storyteller and grounded researcher who is passionate about helping others sort through the numbers to tell real stories and lead positive change. Drawing on her 16 years' teaching experience in Australia and the United Kingdom, she has developed resources to promote data storytelling in schools – including an online self-paced data storytelling course, and the books *Using and Analysing Data in Australian Schools* and *Leading Data-Informed Change in Schools*.

Selena mentors executive leaders, school leaders, middle leaders and teachers in data storytelling, ultimately to benefit the young people that we aim to serve. Selena's third book, *I'm Not a Numbers Person: How to Make Good Decisions in a Data-Rich World*, was published for corporate readers by Major Street Publishing in 2022.

Acknowledgements

Moreso than any of my other books, the contents of this book have been heavily influenced by my work with educators who are innovative, creative and seeking the best for their students, and who are also generous in sharing their practice. Thank you for being willing to share and showcase your extraordinary work – countless other educators will benefit from your generosity.

As always, I have a huge amount of gratitude for my tribe of legends: Tim, Tash, Jhye, Darcy, Carly, Catherine, Al, Dan, Mel, Anna, Liane, Nicola and Geraldine. You lot keep me on the straight and narrow and I appreciate it so much. 😊 Much love to you all.

TLBS, my accountability buddies, my writing crew, and the absolutely majestic Lisa O'Neill – always 'being up to something' is the absolute best.

Brooke, Tess and Alicia… What a #girlgang! It has been so great working with all of you again. You're the best. Thank you.

References

Andrews, RJ (2019), *Info we Trust: How to Inspire the World with Data*, John Wiley & Sons.

Australian Bureau of Statistics (n.d.), 'Statistical language – Quantitative and qualitative data', abs.gov.au/websitedbs/D3310114.nsf/Home/Statistical+Language+-+quantitative+and+qualitative+data.

Australian Institute for Teaching and School Leadership (AITSL) (n.d.), *Learning intentions and success criteria*, aitsl.edu.au/docs/default-source/feedback/aitsl-learning-intentions-and-success-criteria-strategy.pdf?sfvrsn=382dec3c_2.

Berger, J (1972), *Ways of Seeing*, Penguin Books.

Berger, R, Rugen, L, Woodfin, L and Education, EL (2014), *Leaders of Their Own Learning: Transforming Schools Through Student-Engaged Assessment*, John Wiley & Sons.

Berry Street (2023), 'Berry Street Education Model (BSEM)', berrystreet.org.au/learning-and-resources/berry-street-education-model

BEST for the Future (2020), 'BEST self-direction toolkit is live!', best-future.org/2020/11/18/best-self-direction-toolkit-for-grades-k-12-is-live.

Black, P and Wiliam, D (1998), 'Assessment and classroom learning', *Assessment in Education: Principles, Policy & Practice,* 5(1), 7–74.

Bregman, R (2018), *Utopia for Realists: And How We Can Get There*, Bloomsbury Publishing.

Brookhart, SM (2011), 'Tailoring feedback: Effective feedback should be adjusted depending on the needs of the learner', *The Virginia Journal of Education*, 76(9), 33–36.

Brookhart, SM (2017), *How to Give Effective Feedback to your Students*, Association for Supervision and Curriculum Development (ASCD).

Brown, B (2010), *The Gifts of Imperfection: Let Go of Who You Think You're Supposed to Be and Embrace Who You Are*, Simon and Schuster.

Brown, S (2018), 'What is the impact of visual content marketing?', Rocketium, rocketium.com/academy/impact-visual-content-marketing.

Clontarf Foundation (2022), clontarf.org.au.

Cope, B and Kalantzis, M (2016), 'Big data comes to school: Implications for learning, assessment and research', *AERA Open*, 2(2), 1–19.

Doran, GT (1981), 'There's a SMART way to write management's goals and objectives, Management Review, 70(11), 35–36.

Dykes, B (2019), Effective Data Storytelling: How to Drive Change with Data, Narrative and Visuals, John Wiley & Sons.

Einsberg, H (2014), 'Humans process visual data better', Thermopylae Sciences + Technology, t-sciences.com/news/humans-process-visual-data-better.

Fisk, S (2020), *Leading Data-Informed Change in Schools*, Hawker Brownlow Education.

Fisk, S (2022a), *I'm Not a Numbers Person: How to Make Good Decisions in a Data-Rich World*, Major Street Publishing.

Fisk, S (2022b), *Using and Analysing Data in Australian Schools*, 2nd edn, Hawker Brownlow Education.

Hattie, J and Timperley, H (2007), 'The power of feedback', *Review of Educational Research*, 77(1), 81–112.

Heath, C and Starr, K (2022), *Making Numbers Count*, Bantam Press.

Heick, T (2022), '5 Levels Of Student Engagement: A Continuum For Teaching', TeachThought, teachthought.com/pedagogy/levels-engagement.

iDashboards UK (2018), 'People remember only 20% of what they read… But 80% of what they see', Medium, medium.com/@iDashboards_UK/on-average-people-remember-only-20-of-what-they-read-but-80-of-what-they-see-8411224769e2.

Klein, G (2017), *Seeing What Others Don't: The Remarkable Ways we Gain Insights*, Nicholas Brealey Publishing.

Knaflic, CN (2015), *Storytelling with Data: A Data Visualization Guide for Business Professionals*, John Wiley & Sons.

Knapp, MS, Swinnerton, JA, Copland, MA and Monpas-Huber, J (2006), *Data-Informed Leadership in Education*, University of Washington, Center for the Study of Teaching and Policy, education.uw.edu/ctp/sites/default/files/ctpmail/PDFs/DataInformed-Nov1.pdf.

Marzano, RJ (2007), *The Art and Science of Teaching: A Comprehensive Framework for Effective Instruction*, Association for Supervision and Curriculum Development.

Marzano, RJ (2017), *The New Art and Science of Teaching*, Solution Tree Press.

Marzano, RJ and Brown, JL (2011), *A Handbook for the Art and Science of Teaching*, Hawker Brownlow Education.

Monash University (2023), 'Create an exemplar', monash.edu/learning-teaching/teachhq/Teaching-practices/embedding-english-language/how-to/create-an-exemplar.

Pink, DH (2011), *Drive: The Surprising Truth about What Motivates Us*, Penguin.

Schlechty, PC (2002), *Working on the Work: An Action Plan for Teachers, Principals, and Superintendents*, Jossey Bass.

Seife, C (2010), *Proofiness: How you're Being Fooled by the Numbers*, Penguin.

Sharratt, L (2019), *CLARITY: What Matters MOST in Learning, Teaching and Leading*, Corwin Press.

Sharratt, L and Fullan, M (2012), *Putting Faces on the Data: What Great Leaders Do!*, Corwin Press.

Sinek, S (2009), *Start With Why: How Great Leaders Inspire Everyone to Take Action*, Penguin.

Smith, A (2020), 'Narrative writing examples | Bump it up wall', Teach Starter, teachstarter.com/au/blog/narrative-writing-examples-bump-it-up-wall.

Tulchinsky, TH (2018), 'John Snow, Cholera, the Broad Street Pump; Waterborne Diseases Then and Now', in Tulchinsky, TH (ed), *Case Studies in Public Health*, Elsevier.

Visible Learning (2022), 'Hattie ranking: 252 influences and effect sizes related to student achievement', visible-learning.org/hattie-ranking-influences-effect-sizes-learning-achievement.

Zimmerman, BJ and Kitsantas, A (1997), 'Developmental phases in self-regulation: Shifting from process goals to outcome goals', *Journal of Educational Psychology*, 89(1), 29.

www.ingramcontent.com/pod-product-compliance
Lightning Source LLC
Chambersburg PA
CBHW041140110526
44590CB00027B/4078